PITTSBURGH THEO

N

Dikran Y. Hadidian
General Editor

6

THE MYSTICAL SOURCES

OF GERMAN ROMANTIC PHILOSOPHY

THE MYSTICAL SOURCES OF GERMAN ROMANTIC PHILOSOPHY

By

Ernst Benz

Translated by

Blair R. Reynolds and Eunice M. Paul

PICKWICK *Publications* · Eugene, Oregon

Pickwick Publications
An imprint of Wipf and Stock Publishers
199 W 8th Ave, Suite 3
Eugene, OR 97401

The Mystical Sources of German Romantic Philosophy
By Benz, Ernst and Reynolds, Blair R.
Copyright©1983 Pickwick
ISBN 13: 978-0-915138-50-0
Publication date 7/28/2009
Previously published by Pickwick, 1983

CONTENTS

INTRODUCTION

In general, contemporary German existential philosophy takes delight in condemning the philosophy of idealism from Fichte to Schelling as severely as the theologians of the dialectic school condemn Christian mysticism. And that occurs not only in university chairs and church pulpits, but also in philosophical and theological journals, so that mysticism and idealistic philosophy are neglected or even despised subjects.

This situation is not unique to our era: This same phenomenon can already be found at the beginning of the 19th century, when the protagonists of German idealistic philosophy sought to proclaim their new ideas in opposition to the rationalistic philosophy of their times. Franz von Baader, well known in France through the works of Eugene Susini, [1] friend of Hegel and Schelling, professor of the philosophy of religion at the University of Munich, the great champion of the mystical tradition among the philosophers of his time, prepared, in 1813, an edition of Jacob Boehme's works with a general philosophical introduction. But he quickly encountered the sharpest opposition from adherents of traditional rationalism who still occupied the chairs and edited the journals of the time. Baader wrote:

> At the time of my efforts here at Munich to revive the mystical tradition, a certain colleague stated very clearly that--in view of the total confusion provoked in political and religious affairs by men like me--it would be better to beat them to death on the spot. [2]

Indeed, the rationalistic philosophy of the 18th century went to war against a mystical, revolutionary, and disturbing element, which it believed had been removed long ago and of which it spoke only with contempt and disgust. The general attitude of philosophical criticism and modern theology, at least in Germany, is not very far from the conviction of Franz von Baader's colleague, but it is always consoling to know the risks to be run. [3]

1

2

The historical fact of the direct relationships between mystical Christianity, Catholic and Protestant, and German idealistic philosophy was already established through researches on the history of 19th-century philosophy. Friedrich Theodor Vischer, one of the best-known disciples of Hegel, especially in the area of aesthetics, addressed this question to contemporaries:

> Have you forgotten that the new philosophy came forth from the school of the old mystics, especially from Jacob Boehme? [4]

Another disciple of Hegel, Martensen, who published the first book on Master Eckhart's religious speculation, insisted "German mysticism is the first form (Gestalt) in which German philosophy revealed itself in the history of thought." [5] Franz Pfeiffer, who first published the German writings of Master Eckhart--at the suggestion of Franz Baader--wrote in 1845:

> The German mystics are the patriarchs (Erzväter) of German speculation. They represent the beginnings of an independent German philosophy. In short, they embody the principles upon which systems well-known five centuries later were based, not only in their beginnings, but in part already in their totality. [6]

All these witnesses mentioned belong to the second generation of German idealism. They are the disciples of Hegel, Schelling, and Franz von Baader. Later on, the speculative philosophy of the great era of the beginning of the century and its mystical roots were forgotten. It was only at the end of the century that the philosophical historians returned along these tracks. Wilhelm Dilthey, who had a comprehensive vision of the great outlines of the history of the human spirit (Geistesgeschichte) emphasized the continuity of tradition between the German mysticism of the Middle Ages and German idealistic philosophy. [7] After him, it was Heinrich Maier who rediscovered the line of direct communication leading from Master Eckhart to Fichte, Schelling, and Hegel. [8]

All these analyses and suggestions have not succeeded in producing a systematic and methodological investigation of this problem. The studies which follow attempt to clarify this theme.

They represent a kind of synthesis of my earlier studies on some principal thinkers of European mystical theology: Master Eckhart, whose Latin sermons I edited; Jacob Boehme, about whom I published some studies; Swedenborg, in whom I studied the relationships between the ideas he developed during his naturalist, man-of-science period and those mystical ones he formulated during his visionary period; finally, Friedrich Christoph Oetinger, pietism's great theosophist from Würremberg, who so profoundly influenced Hegel, Schelling, and Franz von Baader, and who was at the same time the mystagogue of Jacob Boehme's philosophy and Christian cabalism. [9]

In the following chapters, I will keep the order followed in my lectures on this same theme, given at the College of France in the month of March 1963. They begin with a general introduction on the different literary sources of Christian and non-Christian mysticism in the romantic philosophers, and on the different ways in which these sources penetrated and formed the intuition and speculation of these thinkers. First of all it was necessary to describe the revival of German mysticism from the High Middle Ages, especially that of Master Eckhart, Tauler, **Theologia Deutsch**, and Seuse; next the revival of Jacob Boehme and 18th century spiritual mysticism; the 17th and 18th century rediscovery of theosophy; the direct or indirect influence of Swedenborg's visionary speculation, which was much stronger than was generally imagined; the traces of the cabalistic tradition introduced in Germany by Reuchlin, rediscovered by Oetinger and taken up again by Schelling; and finally the discovery of Indian mysticism, which opened a new era in German idealistic thought.

While the first chapter holds to a rather historical character, the three following chapters will have a more systematic character. First of all, I will speak of the influence of certain well-defined concepts and mystical ideas on idealistic philosophy. We must first make clear the mystical basis of the idealistic concept of reality itself. There are some fundamental concepts, especially in Master Eckhart's theology, which push speculation toward an idealistic view of reality.

The third chapter will be dedicated to a study of the influence of Christian mysticism on Schelling's, Hegel's, and Franz von Baader's philosophies of history.

The fourth chapter will bring to light the presence of the mystical tradition, especially of Oetinger and Christian cabalism, in German idealism's philosophy of nature, particularly in Schelling.

The last chapter is a testimony of thanks for the generous invitation given to me by the College of France. It will be concerned with a French thinker who was the best known, the most widely read, and the most translated of all the French philosophers from the era of German romanticism, the one who influenced, in Germany, all the theological and philosophical circles of the diverse Christian confessions of his time, and who, moreover, justified, in France, the name that he gave himself in his numerous books, the "Unknown Philosopher," since he has remained almost unknown in France until today, Louis Claude de Saint Martin, who seems to me to have a very real importance at a time when we are all seeking a spiritual base for a new Europe.

Chapter One

THE REDISCOVERY OF MYSTICISM

In speaking of the literary sources of mysticism in German idealistic philosophy, we must first of all state a surprising phenomenon: There is a kind of concord and clear convergence of the same sources in almost all the thinkers, in Fichte, in Hegel, in Schelling, in Franz von Baader; we might almost call it "Following a fashion," which made them all turn to the same religious sources of mystical speculation of past centuries, with an almost unconscious spontaneity.

The most exciting phenomenon was the rediscovery of medieval mysticism in the German language in the works of Master Eckhart, Tauler, Seuse, German Theology (Theologia Deutsch) and in the successors of this tradition in the Netherlands, especially Ruisbrook. This rediscovery was expressed in these different philosophers, with an emphatic and sometimes impassioned emotion. The great inspiring force behind this rediscovery of German mysticism at the beginning of the 19th century was Franz von Baader, professor at the University of Munich, founded in 1826 and the center of the idealistic and romantic movement in southern Germany. Baader was the first to discover Master Eckhart's writings, which had been completely eliminated from German and French centers of study after his formal condemnation by the Inquisition's tribunal, first in Cologne, then Rome in 1328. At Munich, Baader read manuscripts of his German sermons and some mystical writings. He was enthralled by them and called Master Eckhart "the central spirit of the religious speculation of the Middle Ages." [10] Until his death, he was preoccupied with Eckhart. Hoffmann, who edited Baader's complete works (and also wrote a biographical introduction to the 16-volume edition), has preserved for us a very interesting conversation about Master Eckhart that he had with Baader a little before the time of the latter's death on April 22, 1841:

> After I suggested to Baader that he should speak about Master Eckhart, by telling him that one of my friends, Dr. Pfeiffer (the well-known Germanist of Munich, who

6

published later, in 1852 the first scientific edition of Master
Eckhart's German writings) was disposed to collect and
edit his works . . . Baader replied: 'In Berlin, I was very
often in Hegel's company. One day, in 1824, I read to
him some of the writings of Master Eckhart, whom he
knew only by name until then. He was so enthused that
I heard him give a whole lecture on Master Eckhart the
other day, and he finished with these words: "Da haben
wir es ja, was wir wollen" (That is exactly what we want,
that is the whole of our ideas, of our intentions).' Baader
continued: 'I tell you, Master Eckhart was called Master
for good reason. He surpasses all the other mystics . . . I
thank God that he deigned to let me know him amid
the philosophical chaos of our time. So the monkeys' screams
against mysticism uttered in a manner so arrogant and
foolish were no longer able to irritate me; and through
him I had access to Jacob Boehme.' [11]

For Baader himself, as well as for Hegel, the importance
of this discovery is obvious. Hegel, introduced personally to Master
Eckhart's ideas by his friend Baader, found in him the verification
and the confirmation of his own philosophy of mind; and Baader
considered him as the most significant inspiration of his own
ideas, and the author who led him directly to that other master
of German mystical speculation, Jacob Boehme. [12] Sharing
the same conviction as Hegel, he found in Master Eckhart the
form of the new metaphysical speculation of his time anticipated
and even already complete. Thus, he wrote in his journal:

If the spirit of speculation in modern times had been oriented towards this theologian and similar minds of the
Middle Ages, without doubt philosophy of religion would
be in a better state. [13]

Baader was convinced that he was charged with the divine mission
of contributing to the revival of philosophy by restoring the mystical tradition to modern philosophical speculation. He began the
introduction to his lectures on speculative dogmatics with the
following words:

I should like to draw your attention to the two causes
of the stagnation which has struck speculative theology
for a long time: the first is the contempt for the efforts
and results of the theory known as mysticism, especially
during the 14th and 15th centuries; and the second is
the contempt for philosophy of religion, or, if you wish,
for Jewish mysticism (that is to say, for the cabala).
I find it all the more necessary to dwell on the first of
these two causes of the decadence of philosophy of religion,
as my own vocation and personal goal is to reintroduce

the forgotten or despised works of this old theory into modern philosophy. Furthermore, I am convinced that the fact of our misjudging and even suppressing the free spirit of the theory has contributed to the division of the church. [14] It was especially these so-called mystics of times past who had adopted the inspired and speculative concept of religion, of which we speak, while the innovators were concerned only with the destruction of this mysticism, that is to say, of speculation . . . Because of that, I believe I render an essential service to today's speculative theology by my efforts to propagate the unacknowledged and lost works of this theory . . . and to demonstrate that the most profound researches of recent times are connected to the earliest ideas. [15] Since almost all Enlightenment philosophy, with its stupefying and stupefied erudition is concerned only with the destruction and total denial of older philosophical and theological institutions, I have taken to heart to foil this destructive philosophy, which conceals its invalidity under the leaves of the vine of critical philosophy while showing traces of this ancient philosophy of nature and religion. [16]

Hegel presented Master Eckhart, in his **Philosophy of Religion**, as one of those rare theologians who had succeeded in exalting religion to the sphere of ideas and abstraction:

If we conceive of the content of the teaching of the church in terms of ideas, or of abstract notions, we will find there the speculative determinations, of which we have spoken; and if there are theologians who are incapable of interpreting such doctrines--which concern, indeed, the most intimate depths of the divine essence--in terms of ideas, or of abstract notions, it would be better for them not to touch it. Theology is the conceptualization of the content of religion; these theologians should confess that they alone would be incapable of conceiving it, and they should not venture to judge the abstract notion by such expressions as pantheism, etc.

There are some ancient theologians who succeeded in conceiving this profundity in the most intimate manner, while for Protestants today, who are concerned only with criticism and history, philosophy and science are entirely irrelevant. Master Eckhart, a Dominican monk, says in one of his sermons: 'The eye with which God looks at me is the eye with which I look at Him, my eye and His eye are identical. In justice, I am weighed in God and He in me. If God did not exist, I would not exist; and if I did not exist, He would not exist either. But it is not necessary to know that, for these are the things which can be easily misunderstood and can be understood only in ideas and abstraction.' [17]

8

Evidently, Hegel discovered the basis for his idealistic interpretation of reality in Master Eckhart's speculations to which his friend Baader introduced him.

The rediscovery of medieval mysticism was not only inspired by romantic sentimentality, it was also a matter of "return to the source" (resourcement), as Father Daniélou says, [18] of speculative inspiration, the creator of German philosophical terminology; and I now feel obliged to make a small philological detour because it is a matter of explaining a German phenomenon, which is strange to French language and literature.

The French language followed normally, step by step, the development of Latin as the philosophical and scientific language. The scholastic philosophy of the Middle Ages, especially in its center, the University of Paris, made Latin a perfect instrument to express in precise and exact terms all developments of logic and abstract thought. The French language shared in this evolution of an exact philosophical terminology: substantia became substance, (substance); identitas became identity (identite). The adaptation of Latin philosophical and scholarly language by the French language progressed naturally and continuously, since the French language is of Latin origin.

In Germany, the situation was completely different. The philosophical and theological language, the language of German schools and universities, was the same Latin as in France, since Latin was the European language of theologians and scholars. No philosophical terminology existed outside Latin disputations, Latin lessons, and Latin scholastic books. On the contrary, the German language of the High Middle Ages was essentially poetic. German literature of the Middle Ages was the literature of the Minnesang, of the troubadours, of the Heldenlied, of epic songs such as the Nibelungenlied, which means that it was a language of images, allegories, parables, not a language of abstract concepts and philosophical and logical terms. There was no philosophical terminology in the German language, and there were no German translations of Latin philosophical or theological treatises. The need did not make itself felt, and the linguistic tool did not exist. The German language of the Middle Ages did not take part in the scholastic development of philosophy, theology, and the sciences.

It is only with German Thomistic mysticism that all this changed, that is to say, with Master Eckhart, professor first at the University of Paris, then at the University of Cologne; and basically it was the German nuns in Dominican convents who provoked the great spiritual revolution, of which we speak, by their ignorance of Latin.

Master Eckhart was the Prior of the Dominican order in the German and Bohemian provinces. As such, he had to visit all the monasteries of his province and preach in the convents. [19] Being learned in Thomistic theology, he had the habit, as had all the preachers of the time, of preaching in Latin; and that meant conceiving his sermons in Latin. Thus, we still have a number of Latin outlines of his sermons with many abbreviations and allusions which are sometimes incomprehensible, his Latin sermon notes from which I have prepared an edition of his sermons, [20] and notes which were the result of his meditations, and which he probably took to the pulpit when he had to preach. These notes are in the traditional style of scholastic theology, with many references and quotations, which are sometimes inexact because they were used from memory, from the Bible, the liturgy, the great theological scholars, and the fathers of the ancient church. [21]

But as Prior of his province, Master Eckhart was also obliged by order of the head of the Order of Saint Dominic, to preach in the convents of the Dominican nuns. Unfortunately for him--these sisters did not know Latin; and thus he had to preach in German. There are many texts of his German sermons, but these texts are in a very frustrating condition since there are variations which are extremely disturbing from a philological point of view. [22] There are notes made by listeners who sometimes transposed the German words of Master Eckhart into their own dialect or gave at least a trace of their own dialect to the notes.

But there is one even more disturbing fact: these German sermons do not correspond to the Latin sermons on the same text of the Gospel for the same Sunday or festival, for which we have Master Eckhart's own notes. There are some resemblances between the Latin and German sermons, but it cannot be said that they are true German translations of the Latin.

The reason for this is that in those days it was not possible for any preacher to translate the Latin notes of a sermon, the result of his hermeneutical and theological meditations in Latin, into German, because for the majority of the Latin theological and philosophical terms there were no corresponding abstract concepts in German. The theological Latin of a sermon's outline was untranslatable.

In these circumstances, for a preacher like Master Eckhart, there were only two ways to make himself understood: either translate the abstract terms of theological language into poetic images, because the German of that time was a language of images; or create a new terminology of abstractions improvised in German. Both these solutions presented difficulties. By transforming Latin scholastic terms into German images, the translator was forced to form some very audacious and dangerous paradoxes, which were capable of being misunderstood and considered as heresies by attentive listeners. On the other hand, the formation of new concepts and unheard-of abstractions in German could make the sermon more or less incomprehensible to listeners who were taken by surprise at these terminological innovations.

Master Eckhart did not escape from either of these two dangers. He was accused of heresy and misunderstood, as is proved by the manuscripts of his German sermons and the excerpts put forward by those who denounced him. [23] At this time, we are interested only in the second point: in the introduction of new philosophical and theological terms into the German language. Master Eckhart is, indeed, the creator of a new German philosophical and theological terminology; and since his own theology was a mystical one, founded on mystical experiences and intuitions, it is truly with mystical speculation that philosophical speculation in German began.

This creation of a German philosophical language was continued later by Jacob Boehme, who himself belonged to the German mystical tradition and was also the author of many other concepts and philosophical or theological terms in German. Indeed, idealistic philosophy avails itself most often of concepts and terms created by Master Eckhart and also his successors such as Tauler and the author of the **Theologia Deutsch,** who were able to avoid the suspicion of heresy and whose writings circulated widely in the intellectual circles of German clergy and laity. All the ontological terms, for example, Sein, Wesen, Wesenheit, das Seiende, das Nichts, Nichtigkeit, nichtigen, all the terms such as Form, Gestalt, Anschauung, Erkenntnis, Erkennen, Vernunft, Vernünftigkeit, Verstand, Verständnis, Verständigkeit, Bild, Abbild, Bildhaftigkeit, entbilden, all the concepts such as Grund, Ungrund, Urgrund, ergründen, Ich, Ichheit, Nicht-Ich, entichen, Entichung are the creations of German mystical speculation; [24] and it is easy to understand why the philosophers of idealism and German romanticism turned again toward this source considering the German mysticism of the Middle Ages as the basis for a "return to the source" (resourcement) of religious philosophy, which was considered the principal task of their own times.

2. The story of the rediscovery of Jacob Boehme by idealistic philosophers is a story even more dramatic and enthralling than the discovery of Master Eckhart. The story of Jacob Boehme's influence on European philosophy is one of the most exciting chapters in the history of European thought. [25] Considering his innate knowledge "insight into the being of all being" ("den Blick ins Wesen aller Wesen" [26]), as a divine revelation accorded to him by a special divine grace, Boehme had pronounced a double

prophecy on the future of his mystical works: First, if the Germans scorned the revelation offered to them in the form of these works, once this spiritual outpouring had passed, they would be obliged to take from foreign nations what they had rejected from him. [27] Also, Jacob Boehme considered his own mystical theology was a sign of the final period of Christian soteriology, as the avant-garde of the "time of lilies," of the Lilienzeit, as the "dawn" of the time when all the prophesies of the final realization of salvation would be fulfilled and when the inner comprehension of the divine revelation would burst forth in the minds of all believers. Boehme declared several times in his spiritual writings that his books would be re-evaluated, rediscovered, and re-established in the time of the lilies, in the time when the Christian revelation would no longer present itself as letter, but as spiritual knowledge, as philosophy of the spirit. [28]

Miraculously, both of these prophecies were realized, not in the direct sense of Boehme, but in a metaphorical one.

The first direct influence of the philosophy of Jacob Boehme on European philosophy did not take place in Germany, but in England, where it could be seen in Isaac Newton's philosophy and Fludd's theosophy, [29] and in the Netherlands, where Amsterdam in particular was a place of refuge for Boehme's disciples persecuted in Germany. Jacob Boehme first returned to Germany because of the effort of the radical groups of spiritualist and separatist pietism in Berlebourg, who translated the English works of the Philadelphians of London, English students of Boehme, into German and furthered, as did Friedrich Christoph Oetinger, a renaissance of Boehmist theosophy by republishing his German works or at least selections from them. [30]

The second great rediscovery of Jacob Boehme, at the beginning of the 19th century, occurred in the same roundabout manner, through "foreign countries," this time through France as intermediary. Jacob Boehme's theosophy was discovered in Alsace by Saint-Martin during his sojourn at Strasburg some years after his initiation into the theosophy of Martinez de Pasqually. [31] Saint-Martin felt that Boehme not only confirmed his own spiritual ideas, which he had received initially from his first tutor Pasqually, but thanks to Boehme he was able to strengthen them to the ultimate intuition, the total vision of being. He did not hesitate to say with a surprising modesty that the works of Jacob Boehme represented the sum of his own writings; and we find in his famous book **Le ministère de l'homme-esprit,** published in 1802, Year XI of the Revolution in Paris, and translated into German in 1845, the following praise of Jacob Boehme:

Furthermore, a German author, whose first two works I have translated and published, namely, **Aurora** and **Die**

> **drei Principien,** can supply amply what mine lack. This
> German author, dead for almost two hundred years, named
> Jacob Boehme, and regarded in his time as the prince
> of theological philosophers, left in his numerous writings,
> which contain almost thirty different treatises, extraordinary
> and astonishing expositions of our primitive nature; of
> the source of evil; of the essence and laws of the universe;
> of the origin of gravity; of what he calls the seven wheels
> or the seven powers of nature; of the origin of water;
> of the nature of the prevarication of the angels of darkness;
> of the nature of man; of the way of reconciliation which
> eternal love employed to reinstate man in his rights, etc. . .
>
> I think I should render a service to the reader by persuading
> him to become acquainted with this author; but urging
> him especially to arm himself with patience and courage
> in order not to become discouraged by the lack of regularity
> in the form of these works, by the abstract nature of
> the matters which he treats, and by the difficulty he
> confesses he had in setting down his ideas, since most
> of the matters under discussion have no analogous words
> in the languages we know. . . .
>
> Reader, if you decide to dip courageously into the works
> of this author, who is judged by so-called scholars to
> be nothing but an 'epileptic,' you will assuredly have no
> need of mine. [32]

Saint-Martin not only delivered this general praise of
Jacob Boehme, who until then had been totally unknown in France,
but he also personally took upon himself the difficult task of
translating some obscure works, full of an entirely new and extraordinary terminology even in German, written in a style that one
would have judged untranslatable into any language, especially
into French. But Saint-Martin succeeded in translating them into
excellent French. [33] Thus, the works of Jacob Boehme were
much more intelligible in the French translation than in their
original language; and we can witness the very curious phenomenon
that several of his works reappeared in German philosophy--espe-
cially in Franz von Baader--in a state of clarification they had
received from their French translation and Saint-Martin's interpretation.

Saint-Martin became the master of a mystical and theosophical school which spread throughout all of Europe as far as
Saint Petersburg and Moscow. Wherever his writings circulated,
he also prepared the way for his own mystagogue and initiator
into theosophy, Jacob Boehme, who was studied even in Russia
and had an enormous influence on the Russian Slavophiles. [34]

It was Franz von Baader again who uncovered Jacob Boehme's theosophy in Germany, at the same time as Saint-Martin. He considered it as his personal mission to re-introduce Jacob Boehme's speculative philosophy into the natural and religious philosophy of his time. In his own relations with Boehme, he underwent a veritable conversion. After his first discovery of Jacob Boehme's work, in his youth, he was so disgusted with the reading that he finished by throwing the volume against the wall of his study with a cry of horror. [35] Later, the "Teutonic philosopher," scorned and mistreated at first, became favorite reading. He gave numerous lectures on Jacob Boehme and prepared an edition of his works, with a general introduction to their ideas and with notes underlining the current importance of his philosophy, all with the intention of leading the German speculative philosophy of his time back to its mystical sources. [36]

To Varnhagen von Ense he wrote: "It gives me great pleasure to scandalize our foolish scholars with this shoe-maker." [37]

Another time he wrote:

> If I call here our 'Teutonic philosopher' the reformer of religious philosophy, I do that in anticipating a not too distant future; and I maintain that the writings and the principles of Jacob Boehme will render excellent service in this purely philosophical reform. I wish to convince at least some capable heads, that in the contemporary idealistic movement of German philosophy, it will no longer be permissible to ignore the writings as being only for the ignorant. [38]

The same Baader is so taken up by Boehme's ideas that he considers himself to be in the light of Boehme's prophecies. The era of idealistic theology, of which he flatters himself to be the initiator, appears to him as the realization and accomplishment of Boehme's prophecies, the "imminent time of the lilies." Baader says:

> Without doubt, the time of the lilies, of which Boehme speaks so often, and when his own writing will be, he said, accepted and esteemed, has already begun. [39]

We find similar judgments in other philosophers of German idealism, and we sense the great emotion aroused by the rediscovery of Boehme's mystical theology. Hegel himself was a follower of Boehme from his youth, and he boasted of it sometimes in his works and letters. [40] Schelling is more reserved in his books; he does not like to reveal his sources and name his spiritual ancestors. But his letters are more frank. In a letter to his father on September 7, 1806, he writes that Franz von Baader has asked

9/07

him to obtain for him the writings of his compatriot, the theosopher Friedrich Christoph Oetinger, and that Schelling himself has conveyed this desire to his friend Pregizer, who was a disciple of Oetinger. Pregizer, who was the founder of a pietistic sect called "the Joyous Christians," recalls in this response to Schelling that Oetinger and Jacob Boehme had been the principal subject of their conversation on the occasion of their meeting in 1803 in Murrhardt. [41]

In general, Schelling's correspondence proves very clearly that there was a very active exchange of mystical literature among the leaders of German idealistic philosophy. We find Schelling occupied with obtaining for his friend Baader, thanks to the help of his friend Schubert, the famous author of the book on the soul, a copy of **Cherubinischer Wandersmann**, by Angelus Silesius, which transcribed all the mystical theology of Eckhart and of Tauler into epigrams (Sinngedichte). The same Schelling requests his friend Schubert to procure for him an old edition of Tauler's writings, "not a modern revision, but an edition as old as possible, which has faithfully retained all the particular characteristics of the author. For these writings are almost as important for the study of our language as they are for that of mysticism, and they are also as potent for richness of literary expression as for quickening of the mind." These extracts from Schelling's and Baader's letters show us they were perfectly conscious of the importance of German mystical tradition in their own efforts to create a philosophical terminology adequate for the expression of their idealistic theories. [42]

3. In a similar manner, the work of Emmanuel Swedenborg, the Swedish visionary, was discovered and adopted by the idealistic philosophers. Swedenborg's work was closely linked to the works of Jacob Boehme and Saint-Martin as much in the theosophical tradition of German pietism as in the tradition of Christian freemasonry in Germany and Russia. Swedenborg's visionary theology was introduced into Germany in the second half of the 18th century by the founder of German theosophy, whom we have just mentioned as the principal propagandist of Boehme's ideas among the pietistic circles of Württemberg, Friedrich Christoph Oetinger. [43] Oetinger was in correspondence with Swedenborg; he was the first to translate some of Swedenborg's Latin works into German, and by his writings contributed much to dissipate the suspicion of heresy the theologians of Lutheran orthodoxy formulated against Swedenborg's ideas and visionary experiences.

Oetinger considered the Swedish visionary's revelations as a true continuation and augmentation of biblical revelation, adding to it specific theories about the spiritual and celestial worlds. For his part, Oetinger compared Swedenborg's system with Boehme's mystical theology on the one hand, and on the other with the philosophy-of-nature systems of the great natural-science scholars, such as Newton, Baglive, and Cluver. Since the central problem of the human personality's nature and value was posed so vigorously by the idealistic philosophers, they were obliged to be concerned also with the problems of survival, of the continuation of life after death and its future evolution, and especially with the problem of the future of the personal relationships of love, marriage and friendship beyond the tomb. The great dramas of friendship, love, and marriage in the circles of idealistic philosophers and German romantic poets are comprehensible only against the background of this philosophical and poetical discussion inspired by Swedenborg, who displays all the symptoms of impassioned emotion. [44]

The most important event which put this theme of the survival of love after death in the center of the theological and philosophical discussion, and which especially intensified Swedenborg's interest, was the unexpected death of Karoline, Schelling's wife, in 1811. This death, which deprived the philosopher of his wife and confidant, destroyed an amorous liaison whose dramatic and sometimes scandalous history had been followed by all the intellectual, literary, and university circles of the time in Germany with the greatest attention. At Mayence, Karoline had enthusiastically taken part in the events of the French Revolution; she returned from Mayence with living proof of her enthusiasm, her daughter, whose father was an officer of the French Revolutionary Army. August Schlegel saved her by offering marriage, but that lasted only until Schelling entered her life.

We must add that the official divorce of Karoline from her previous husband, August Schlegel, was the first and at that time almost the only consequence of the French Revolution on German soil. The Duke of Weimar was the first German sovereign to introduce civil marriage and divorce into his country despite the vehement opposition of the clergy; and it was his famous minister Goethe, who interceded in favor of Karoline, August Schlegel and Schelling and, as minister responsible, with the permission of his Duke, for the first time in Germany, ratified that notorious divorce. It is very strange to see Goethe act as minister in an affair which brought the spirit of the revolution into play. By this act, Goethe was to some degree the material and spiritual cause of the uprising of idealistic philosophy, since Karoline became the inspiration of Schelling's great visions and theories, and the center of the circle of writers and philosophers who assembled around them both. [45]

After Karoline's unforeseen and unexpected death in the wake of a cholera attack during a visit to Schelling's parents at Maulbronn, far away from him, Schelling engaged in incessant speculations on the possibility of maintaining contact with his dear departed. In this situation, denying the separation forced by death, Swedenborg's ideas, in which he maintained the continuation of true marriage after death and the perfecting of our marital and loving relationships in the heavenly kingdom, provided him with a unique consolation in the grievous suffering at the separation. Schelling expressed his ideas on the survival of our loves and our friendships beyond the tomb in a philosophical dialogue, Clara; oder, Zusammenhang der natur mit der geisterwelt, (or the Relationships Between the Natural World and the Spiritual World), a dialogue written in very poetic language and full of insights inspired by his recent grievous experience. [46] But the same ideas are to be found in the elderly Schelling, **Die welt-alter** . . . (The Ages of the World); and until the end of his life he remained receptive to Swedenborg's ideas on the spiritual world and on the organization of the spiritual life in the heavenly world and in other worlds.

There is a letter from Schelling, written on March 19, 1811, to his friend Georgii, who had recently lost his wife and to whom Schelling, still crushed by the loss of Karoline, wrote the following words:

> My continual meditation and my incessant researches have only served to confirm my conviction that death, far from debilitating the personality, rather strengthens it, by liberating it from many contingencies, and that the word 'remembrance' is much too weak an expression to designate the inner consciousness the dead one keeps of his former life and of those he has left behind . . . and that we remain united with them in our innermost being, since at our best we are nothing more than they are themselves-- spirits, and that for souls united in sentiment and spirit, souls which have had during their life only one love, only one faith, only one hope, a future reunion is a certain thing, and above all that there are no promises of our Christian religion which will not be fulfilled, however difficult to understand they may be for our reason which uses only abstract terms. Day by day, I become more aware that everything holds together in a much more personal and infinitely more vivid way than we could imagine. If there were still something lacking in the certitude of these convictions, it would require only the death of a person dearly loved and intimately united with us to increase it to the greatest intensity. [47]

Finally, a few words on the discovery of Indian mysticism. There is an excellent book by Father de Lubac (1952) [48] on the encounter of Buddhism and the West, a book which is especially concerned with the reactions of French literature and philosophy to this event. There is another German book, by Helmut von

Glasenapp, **Das Indienbild deutscher Denker** (1960), **[49]** which describes the influence of Indian literature and especially Indian religious philosophy on German literature and philosophy. I will limit myself to a few remarks on the encounter with the spiritual tradition of India at the time of idealistic philosophy, which coincides with the time of the first discoveries of this tradition in Germany.

In general, one can say that at that time in Germany, a real understanding of Vedic or Buddhist literature was very rare, but from the little that was known some daring perceptions and insights were extracted. In Germany, it was Herder who first realized the prime importance of this Indian spirituality heretofore unknown, which was beginning to spread out to Europe. [50] After him came Friedrich Schlegel who uttered the decisive word, in his book, **Über die Sprache und Weisheit der Inder.** Schlegel was convinced the discovery of Indian literature would be an extraordinary source of inspiration and fruitfulness for German philosophy, similar to that brought about by the rediscovery of classical antiquity at the time of the Renaissance. [51]

The reaction to this work was exceptionally strong and favorable. In Novalis we read:

> Fern im Osten wird es helle,
> Graue Zeiten werden jung. [52]

Schelling gloated: "Die Vorzeit hat sich weider aufgetan" ("Antiquity is revealed once again"); and he regarded Indian mysticism as an essential confirmation of his own admiration for mysticism. Mysticism appeared then as the universal theology, the primordial theology, the theology of Adam, as the common spiritual base of all religions. This discovery encouraged philosophers and poets from the time of Herder and Hamann up to Schlegel, Schelling, and Baader to proclaim again the idea of a universal and primordial revelation given at the beginning of time to all mankind. It seemed unthinkable to ignore all that was offered in these Indian works with regard to Europe, by denouncing them simply as pagan. [54]

Friedrich Schlegel returned to the idea of a universal revelation in order to explain Indian philosophy. He said:

> Considered as a natural evolution of reason . . . the Indian
> system is perfectly inexplicable. There are great errors
> in it, but everywhere traces of divine truth. We have
> no desire to deny the ancient Indians knowledge of the
> true God. What should arouse our surprise and astonishment
> even more is the belief in the immortality of the soul
> and the sublime idea of the incarnation, another proof

of the profundity of the Indian mind and the high degree
of its wisdom. [55]

The idealistic philosophers found their own idealistic
interpretation of reality in this Indian philosophy and stated with
surprise "that all Oriental philosophy," as Schlegel said, "could
be called idealism."

> Furthermore . . . the real agreement with what in European
> philosophy is called idealism consists in the fact that in
> this vision activity, life, and liberty are recognized as
> the only true reality . . . while dead immobility and inert
> immutability are rejected as vain and futile. [56]

Until then, they were convinced they had found the prototype
of idealistic philosophy in the Greeks; but now, they were discovering a much more ancient and vigorous form of idealism in the
ancient Orient, of which Schlegel said:

> Even the supreme philosophy of Europeans, the idealism
> of reason (der Idealismus der Vernunft), as the ancient
> Greeks formed it, compared with the abundance of strength
> and light of Oriental idealism, would seem like only a
> weak Promethian spark alongside the full celestial ardor
> of the sun. [57]

However, this idealistic religion of India was mystical,
since union or reunion with God was its goal. Thus, German idealism
found its own inner propensity to mysticism confirmed to an
unexpected degree by the discovery of Indian mysticism.

German idealistic philosophers discovered another confirmation of their interpretation of Indian mysticism, in Saint-Martin,
who was himself one of the first to confer epoch-making importance
to the recent discovery of Indian philosophy. In his **Ministère
de l'homme-esprit**, we find the following lines which I shall take
the liberty of quoting because the "Unknown Philosopher" remained
unknown, even to Father de Lubac:

> Perhaps the time is not far off when Europeans will cast
> their eyes eagerly upon objects which the majority of
> them envision only with suspicion or even contempt. Their
> scientific structure is not firm enough not to have to
> submit to several changes before long. . . The literary
> riches of Asia will also come to their aid. When they
> see the countless treasures that Indian literature is beginning
> to offer us, when they peruse everything promised to
> us by the Asiatic Research Society of Calcutta, the Mahab-
> barat,--a collection of sixteen epic poems containing 100,000
> stanzas on the mythology, religion and ethics of the Indians,

and on their history; the Oupnek'hat, translated by M. Anquetil, which contains extracts of the Vedas, etc., they will be struck by the connections they see between Eastern opinions and those of the West on the most important points. Some will be able to search out in this mine the resemblances of languages by the alphabets, inscriptions, and monuments. Others will be able to find there the bases of all the prodigious theology of the Egyptians, Greeks, and Romans. Finally, still others will find striking similarities to all the dogmas published for several centuries by the various spiritualists of Europe, which they never suspected had been learned in India. [58]

Chapter Two

THE MYSTICAL SOURCES OF SOME FUNDAMENTAL
IDEAS OF GERMAN IDEALISM

The German idealistic philosophers were not all idealists in the proper sense of the word. There is not only a remarkable difference between the idealistic concept of the various systems, from Kant and Fichte to Hegel and Schelling, but these philosophers themselves passed through an evolution in their own principal ideas. Schelling, in particular, very quickly went beyond his purely idealistic phase and returned to a more realistic interpretation of the universe, or more exactly what he termed ideal-realism (Idealrealismus).

However, all these thinkers have traits in common; and the word "idealism" is still the simplest formula to express the specific characteristic of this group of thinkers. The formula is just as true and just as false as most generalizations of this kind.

The essential characteristic of German idealistic philosophy is that objects of reality themselves are no longer considered to be the basis for the interpretation of reality, but the consciousness of man, the mind, having become conscious of itself in him, the Self. Idealistic philosophy progresses from the basis of classical ontology to the discovery of the human personality as the center of all knowledge and action. The absolute, seen by philosophers of preceding centuries as in a transcendent hereafter far away from us, becomes real in the consciousness of man, in the mind conscious of itself, in the Self. The intellectual act is understood as a creative act of the Self, in which the Self, according to the philosophy of Fichte, "establishes" (setzt) the world. God, the absolute and universal law, becomes real in the human mind; the absolute mind, according to Hegel, reaches consciousness and realization in man. The world of the mind and spirit is no longer, as in Descartes, a world of abstractions, but a tangible manifestation of God, as in the opinion of Master Eckhart. [59]

21

This decisive step in modern philosophy was prepared by mysticism and especially by the mystical doctrine of "the spark of the soul" or "in the soul," scintilla in anima, the Seelenfunken, as Master Eckhart taught. [60]

This idea is not new in him; it came from the Thomistic ontology taught at the University of Paris, the center for Thomism in the High Middle Ages. Die Wacht am Sein, of which Gabriel Marcel spoke so favorably, has much more ancient traditions in Paris than in Cologne or in Fribourg. However, in Master Eckhart, this idea of the spark of the soul has a particular meaning; for him it is not an intellectual discovery, but is born of the personal mystical experience, of the individual experience in the union of the mystic with God. We cannot doubt the legitimacy of this experience, even if we have not encountered it ourselves. The history of Christian mysticism shows us that this experience is a fact, independent of all theories on the possibility and legitimacy of that fact.

By this idea of the spark in the soul, Master Eckhart strives to reconstruct this experience of union by intellect, in logical categories, to give an explanation and rational interpretation for it. It is a general rule and a typically human phenomenon that each true religious experience, each encounter of man with God, which, in general, we first feel as an experience surpassing our normal senses and habitual concepts, then we seek to explain it and to verify its origin and development and its psychological or metaphysical presuppositions. Thus, Master Eckhart developed the idea of Seelenfunken in order to explain or interpret his experience of union with God.

What does this term the spark in the soul mean? There is something innate in the created human soul: "the stronghold in the soul," "the summit of the soul," "the apex of the soul," "the spark in the soul." It is in this spark that the union between God and man is realized, that God and the soul touch. In this spark, God Himself engenders His Son; there He becomes totally real; there He enters with all the plentitude of His being.

But Master Eckhart described this experience of union, which becomes real in the spark of the soul, not only from the side of God as the invasion or outpouring of God into the human soul, but also from the side of man as man's elevation and ascension through this "apex" to the point where the soul thus elevated and exalted participates not only in the inner life of God, but also in his activity as creator and Savior.

In this bold idea which says that the mystic, in his state of union with God, himself performs the creative work of God, the decisive step, which we just mentioned, appears; the act by which the basis of the understanding of reality is transferred from the divine transcendence into the human soul, into the spark of the soul, into the summit of intellect, into the intellectual act itself. Master Eckhart says:

> There is a force in the soul which operates only by making it one with God. It creates and makes all with God and has nothing in common with anything else. It begets with the Father the same only son--denselben engeborenen Sohn. Where time never entered, where the rays of images never entered, in the most intimate and sublime depths of the soul, there, God creates the entire world. All that God created--6,000 years ago--and all that God will continue to create in the next millenium if the world continues to exist that long, God creates all that in the most intimate and sublime depths of the soul. All the past and all the future, God creates in the inmost depths of the soul. [61]

In these words we find the first allusion to the idealistic doctrine according to which the absolute creative spirit becomes real in the human soul, which then gives up its own particular being and becomes pure:

> In the eternal birth, the soul becomes pure and one. Thus, its existence is the same as God's. This existence is the beginning of each work of God in the heavens and on the earth. It is the origin (Ursprung) and source of all divine works. [62]

Eckhart goes even one step further toward idealistic philosophy: in the soul, that is to say, in this supreme act of consciousness, realized in the mystical union, man creates himself. Eckhart speaks of a Selbstschöpfung, "self-creation" of man. Eckhart says:

> I was my first cause, I was the cause of myself; there, I wished myself and I wished nothing other; I was what I wished, and what I wished was I. For in this essence of God, in which he is beyond all essence and all differ-ence, there I was myself and I recognized myself as creator of this man; and because of that, I am the cause of myself according to my being which is eternal, but not according to my becoming which is temporal; and because of that, I am ungeboren--a being which was never born--and thus I can never die. [63]

In this audacious and paradoxical attempt of Eckhart to give an intellectual explanation of his mystical experience, the traditional attributes of God are transferred into the attributes of a deified or more than deified self, since it has become identical with the only Son of God born in the soul. The mystic who is part of the intelligible world and its creative forces discovers that he himself is the creative source, and that in the sense of being creator of his own being, in the center of the universe.

But let us not forget that these ideas of Master Eckhart are very tentative attempts at an interpretation and understanding of his own mystical experience, and that they are the bold intellectual expression of a sublime mystical exaltation experienced perhaps rarely in his life, which lifted him beyond the consciousness of his existence as a creature and led him into the arms of God.

However, for this intellectual interpretation of his mystical experience, Eckhart prepared a form of thought which was developed later by idealistic philosophy to become the idea of the Self-creator and the creative force of the mind of the Self, which "establishes" the world and which "establishes itself."

We could show that this idealistic concept of the Self in Fichte is directly influenced by the theories of German mysticism of the Middle Ages, as von Bracken proved in his book on Fichte and Master Eckhart. [64] But we also find in Franz von Baader the same evidences of a direct connection with the old mystical traditions. He takes the same doctrine of the spark of the soul and the birth of the Son in the soul as the point of departure for his speculations. He firmly denounces the opinion, already prevalent at that time, that the proper intent of mysticism would be to suffocate and destroy the Self in the experience of the union. Baader says:

> If the mystics speak of a submersion of the creature in God, they speak only of the abolition, abrogation, or the suppression of the bad Selbheit, of the bad personality, of the bad Self; and that means that in this abrogation (Aufhebung) (of the bad self) the true self, the true personality (die wahre Selbheit) becomes the bond of the union. [65]

That is to say, in this mystical union with God, the absolute and universal Self, the mystic loses his bad self, his limited ego, his limited "myself," in order to receive in the union his universal Self, the image of God, the only Son:

> God exalts himself immediately in the self by the power of his divinity to the extent that the self ultimately exalts itself by the power of the true self. [65a]

Baader then expresses the same idea in the words of Tauler, in which the experience of God's birth in the soul is already interpreted in an idealistic sense:

> Man can be good only by participating in the divine nature.
> That only happens when the God living above the world
> descends in him in this world, that is to say, when this
> God becomes incarnate in him.

> 'Ewig strebst du umsonst, Dich dem Göttlichen ähnlich
> zu machen,
> Hast Du das Göttliche nicht erst zu dem Deinem gemacht.'

> Your efforts to be assimilated into the divine will be vain
> for all eternity, if you have not first appropriated the
> divine to yourself, that is to say, if the source of creative
> genius does not spring in you yourself.

The mystic who experiences union with God and who, in this union, participates in the creative work of God is understood by the idealistic philosopher as the genius whose creative genius reflects the fact that the absolute spirit becomes real in him in the "central vision," the Blick ins Wesen aller Wesen.

This interpretation of genius is the result of a transformation, which can only be considered from a theological point of view as a sign of a progressive secularization. In the generation following Sturm und Drang the concept of genius had already been detached from its Christian context. But even in this case, genius understood in the true idealistic sense is the heir of the mystical and the "central vision" of idealistic philosophy in the direct reflection of the mystical experience. Finally, the terminology of religious idealistic philosophy itself is drawn consciously from the language of the mystics, in which they interpreted their mystical experience of divinization. It is not by chance that Fichte not only developed his ideas in systematic treatises, but also in his **Anweisung zum seligen Leben** (Introduction to the blessed life; or Spiritual Guide to the blessed life). [66] The title is reminiscent of the literary tradition of mysticism, which produced a great number of "spiritual guides" read especially in German pietistic circles--a series which commences with the translation of **The Spiritual Guide** of Miguel de Molinos, by August Hermann Francke, founder of German pietism, and which finishes with Fichte in the idealistic interpretation of the mystical experience as an experience of the immersion of the self liberated from all self will and from all egocentricism, into the pure divine being.

Chapter Three

ESCHATOLOGY AND THE PHILOSOPHY OF HISTORY

If we compare the general attitude of German idealistic philosophers with that of thinkers of the preceding generation, we are struck not only by a new tendency toward speculation, by aspiration to a superior unity of reason and divine revelation, by the tendency to elevate faith to the level of a vision, of an "observation," of an intellectual intuition, but also by the fact that German idealism does not constitute merely a renewal on the theoretical level of the philosophy of religion or of the philosophy of nature of German mysticism: it includes also its own eschatological element, its own way of relying on history, an attempt at the elucidation of the meaning of existence by means of an interpretation of history. This interpretation of history moreover does not depend on an interpretation of the past and the present; it has the impetus of a prophecy enduring until the end of time; it is centered on the idea of a completion, of an end of history. Neither Schelling, Hegel, nor Franz von Baader seek to conceal the theological backgrounds of this problem when, in their metaphysic of history, they speak of "the Kingdom of God," "the conclusion of time," "the Last Judgment," and the "End of Time."

This fundamental characteristic, the idea of an "End of Time," dominates to such a degree that it will find a prolongation in those disciples of idealistic philosophy for whom the idealistic interpretation of history changed into a materialistic one. This fundamental eschatological characteristic appears again very clearly in Marx's dialectical materialism, with the difference that here "the Golden Age," or the "Reign of a Thousand Years" are replaced by Communistic society, and the role of the redemptor is transferred from Christ to the Proletariat. That is a complex problem much debated in France. [68]

This new interpretation of history is already expressed in the first outlines of Schelling's metaphysic of history--which he set down in his **System des transcendentalen Idealismus.** [69]

27

By way of a conclusion to his critique of the various conceptions of history, he writes:

> From the preceding, the only true interpretation of history follows naturally. Taken as a whole, history is a continual and progressive revelation of the absolute. We are never able, then, to determine the precise point in the course of history where the stamp of Providence or God himself becomes visible, so to speak. For God never is, if he is called upon to be that which manifests itself in the objective world; if he was, we would not be; but he does not cease to reveal himself. By his history, man furnishes a continual proof of God's existence, but a proof which only history in its totality can bring to term.

Similarly, later, Schelling, in his **Vorlesungen über die Methode des theologischen Studiums,** developed the idea that Christianity had been necessary to suggest to humanity the meaning of the absolute significance of the historical process, whereas Antiquity knew only the eternity of the world:

> Christianity too, in its depths, is historical in the most exalted sense of the term. Each particular instant of time is the revelation of a particular aspect of God, and he is in each of them absolutely.

Finally, the universe in its totality is also envisioned from a historical angle:

> The absolute relationship consists of the fact that in Christianity the universe in its totality . . . is considered in a historical manner. [70]

In Hegel, this fundamentally historical conception of being reappears. In the well-known postulates of the preamble to his **Phänomenologie des Geistes** we read:

> The True is the whole. But the whole is nothing other than the essence consummating itself through its development. Of the Absolute it must be said that it is essentially a result, that only in the end is it what it truly is." [71]

A similar idea appears in the equally well-known lines on absolute knowledge in the final chapter of the **Phänomenologie:**

> But this substance which is Spirit is the process in which Spirit becomes what it is in itself; and it is only as this process of reflecting itself into itself that it is in itself truly Spirit. It is in itself the movement which is cognition . . . The movement of carrying forward the form

> of its self-knowledge in the labor which it accomplishes
> as actual History. [72]

> History is a conscious self-mediating process--Spirit emptied
> out into Time.

In this alienation:

> . . . the Spirit displays the process of its becoming Spirit
> in the form of free contingent happening . . .

Then, history appears as:

> . . . the Calvary of absolute Spirit, the actuality, truth,
> and certainty of his throne, without which he would be
> lifeless and alone. Only from the chalice of this realm
> of Spirits, foams forth for Him his own infinitude. [73]

Eschatology, this fundamental trait of idealistic thought responds to a new stage of historical consciousness, unknown to Enlightenment philosophy. This new stage had been reached in Germany, thanks to an outburst of apocalyptic sentiment, which our own apocalyptic era has made us understand anew, and which touches the whole of German pietism, but more particularly the Swabian pietists Bengel and Oetinger.

The Swabian fathers are well-known in Paris thanks to the lectures given by Robert Minder at Jean Wahl's school of philosophy and at the College of France. [74]

Johann Albrecht Bengel lived from 1687 to 1752. He was the administrator of the Protestant high school in Denkendorf and later dean of the Protestant clergy in Herbrechtingen. His three principal works are a critical edition of the original Greek text of the New Testament, prepared on the basis of a comparison of all the manuscripts available at the time (**Gnomon** 1752), and particularly his **Erklärte Offenbarung Johannis oder vielmehr Jesu Christi** (1740), and his **Sechzig erbauliche Reden** (1746). [75]

The most well-known of his followers was Friedrich Christoph Oetinger, dean of the Protestant clergy at Weinsberg and Herrenberg and later prelate at Murrhardt. His principal work was **Theologia ex idea vitae deducta** (1765) and a series of other theological treatises and sermons.

He was in personal contact with the radical pietistic groups of his time, the cabalistic groups of Frankfurt, the separatist groups of Berlebourg, which he visited in 1721-31, and the Moravian societies and their founder, Count Zinzendorf, whom he visited at Hernhutt in 1733.

These two theologians directly influenced Schelling, Hegel, and Hölderlin, who were students at the Stift in Tübingen, the famous seminary for students of Protestant theology. [76]

Fuhrmanns for one, [77] has attempted an interpretation of Schelling's philosophy which places him within the totality of the purely philosophical development of his time without taking into consideration the theological and mystical sources of his speculations; but, as we will see, his principal ideas are dependent upon the terminology of Bengel and Oetinger in such a direct and visible way that it is impossible to ignore these fundamental sources of his thought.

These relationships will be even more evident after the appearance of an edition of the complete works of Oetinger, which is in preparation. [78]

For J. A. Bengel, the experience of the apocalyptical character of his own era was decisive. His youth was marked by the wars of Louis XIV, by repeated and cruel occupations of his native city, which was burned, and by no less numerous periods of exile. Consequently, the evolution in the spiritual order appeared to him like a "sign of the times," the announcer of the approaching end of history: the violent attacks of the Counter-Reformation against German Protestantism in the East and West, the rationalistic thrust, the appearance of a materialistic and atheistic philosophy, which from this time on began to be popular, the intrusion of a rationalistic critique of the Bible and dogmas even within the Church, the birth of a new type of political man (according to him, men placing themselves beyond all good and evil) in the autocratic princes of his time--all this made him see the history of his own era as a rapid march toward the culminating point of the struggle between Christ and Antichrist. [79]

Now, if his experience compelled him toward a consideration of the present centered upon the idea of redemptive history, it also obliged him by the same token to place his era in the context of this providential history. For Bengel, the general unfolding of universal history constitutes an organic unity, a system determined by a fixed divine plan of redemption, or as he says in the language of ancient soteriology, by a "divine economy." He finds his information about the nature of this economy in Holy Scripture, the books of which are not to be considered as:

> . . . simple collections of maxims and examples, as scattered
> vestiges of Antiquity, out of which one would find it difficult
> to construct a whole, but as the incomparable proclamation
> of the Economy of that which concerns human nature,
> from the beginning to the end of all things, through all
> the epochs of the world, as a beautiful system and majesti-

cally one . . . One single idea traverses all . . . what
God makes real by the intermediary of a few saints, and
what he makes real by the intermediary of all his people
is miraculously intertwined, and a single glance at the
divine economy, which comprises all things, says more
to us than the confused instructions and the fashionable
scholarly speculations in the studies of the world's powerful. [80]

Here we see to what degree already the consideration
of faith is oriented toward history. History is the true domain
for the realization of his idea in a "System majestically one."
History is the place where God revealed himself concretely--was
incarnate; and the knowledge of God is a glance into the secrets
of his economy. Theological knowledge is a knowledge of History.
This also permits us to understand why Bengel insists on a historical
and contextual commentary on Scripture, for Scripture is:

. . . an inventory of God's community from the beginning
to the end of the world, where the origin, the course
and final objective of the world, of human nature and
the community of God are described, also the continual
revelation of the living God by his works and words, in
his almightiness, justice, and mercy.

Holy Scripture contains:

. . . a continuing testimony basing all the unity of Scripture
upon times gone by, dominated by sin . . . ; this testimony
is to culminate on the great day when our Lord Jesus
Christ appears; and it is only then that all these pages
will assume their true importance. [80a]

These lines confirm the insistence with which Bengel
clings to this inner cohesion, which in the providential plan of
God binds together the Bible and the history of the world. For
him, Holy Scripture encompasses the totality of the processes
of the history of providence from the beginning to the end of
the world, the origin, the course and the final objective of the
history of God's community. Thus, history and Holy Scripture
are intimately bound together, history makes real the divine providential plan; but the ways of its progress are inaccessible to
the natural man who can only suffer the assault of the events
of his own time--contradictory events without any apparent order,
whose inner consistency he cannot fathom. But Holy Scripture
harbors the total plan of the whole of providential history. In
it, the rules according to which God reveals himself in the course
of time, the laws according to which he has arranged his economy,
the goal assigned to the courses he pursues, and the scales of
values according to which he judges human works are revealed

to man. The revelation of God in Holy Scripture is thus, at its deepest, the revelation of his action in history; and it is necessary to make history appear as a totality, as a "system," as an organic order.

Furthermore, to this idea of economy a second one is attached, which reappears also in the historical metaphysics of German idealism, the idea of development or evolution. Already, in Bengel, it has taken a stand against the rationalist idea of progress. In the citation above, Bengal indicates that in the divine inventory, Holy Scripture, the "progressive revelation of the living God through his works and through his words" is related. Thus, a developmental process of revelation is made real in history. In Bengel, this basic idea of ancient soteriology took a new form, which is not without significance. There is, in the course of history, a development of revelation. Contrary to the concept of orthodox dogmatism, which puts the accent on the "once-ness" and the definitive fulfillment of the Revelation, Bengel clung to the idea of successive stages in the development of Revelation.

We can now understand how Bengel's most eminent disciple, F. C. Oetinger, also understood this idea of a progressive revelation in the sense that the revelation continues beyond the canonical connection of the New Testament. Oetinger saw in the arrival on the scene of great visionaries such as Engelbrecht and Swedenborg, and the rediscovery of great mystics such as Jacob Boehme, an authentic continuation of the Revelation, not as complementary to the Bible, but as a new light on its profound meaning. [81] He was able to make use of his teacher, Bengel, precisely on this point. In Bengel, also, the idea of a development of revelation in the course of history is tied to the idea of a progression in the interpretation of Holy Scripture. Scripture's total content in its complexity is not comprehensible and accessible to every epoch; each epoch draws up its own interpretation; but in the course of the centuries a development in the understanding of Scripture comes about. As history and the Bible are linked to each other, we can follow in the course of history an evolution according to history (that is to say, according to the Bible), of the interpretation of Scripture and, if one may say so, of their self-interpretation. History being the history of redemption--soteriology--and Holy Scripture holding encoded within itself the whole plan of the history of redemption, historical progress leads to progress in the deciphering of Holy Scripture. Oetinger dared to condense this idea in a bold statement: "We are better equipped than the apostles." [82]

Bengel had put into practice this idea of the historical development of revelation in his interpretation of The Revelation according to Saint John. Saint John's book of the Apocalypse took on for him, by virtue of his idea of Scripture as "inventory of the world," an exceptional importance to the point of becoming in his eyes the most important book of the whole Bible. This book is in some way a "manifest" of the Lord of History, in which all the unfolding of the history of the Kingdom of God from the coming of Christ to his return is related. [83] Here, the relationships between revelation and history appear extremely clearly; since the whole history of the Kingdom of God is contained in The Revelation according to Saint John, history itself engages in a continual deciphering of this Apocalypse:

> It is expedient, therefore, to entrust its true sense to this word 'revelation,' not as that of a sudden revelation, but as a movement by degrees, from one epoch to another, of the history of the church, and equally in certain souls from one experience to another . . . Everything is but a permanent accomplishment of revelation, from the Sunday when John, at Patmos, saw it and described it down to our own time and on until the Last Judgment. All that, when brought together, constitutes a single coherent History. [84]

Bengel reduces the historical process to the following simple formula: "Revelation happens by degrees until the moment when it reaches us." [85] Those degrees can be seen in the course of history itself as well as in its theological interpretation. The successive sections of Scripture remain mute until the time for their deciphering comes:

> The servants of God are at home throughout the whole extent of the divine abode, and everything is open to them, but each thing in its own time. [86]

This idea of development by degrees has been thoroughly explored by Oetinger. Following this idea, Bengel also boldly adopts the theory of the historical development of revelation. Indeed, he feels honored by a particular revelation, consisting of the fact that, by virtue of a special grace, the true key to the chronological calculation of the history of salvation has been offered him. If the Apocalypse contains the total unfolding of the history of the Kingdom of God, if the course of the history of the church is symbolically represented in the succession of persons and events in the Apocalypse of Saint John, it should then be possible to establish a chronological relationship between the succession of historical events and the succession of personages and episodes in the Apocalypse. Bengel himself was firmly convinced that he had discovered this relationship and did not hesitate to ascribe this discovery to a personal divine inspiration.

The number of the "Beast," 666, which was the basis of his other chronological calculations, figured in his eyes as

of a special divine grace. The intuition regarding the chronology
of The Revelation according to Saint John came to him when
he was preparing his sermon for the first of December 1724.
The revelation came to him of the temporal and non-onomastic
character of the number of the Beast, 666, a number referring
to the period when the church was dominated by the Beast, from
1143 until 1809. [87]

   The result of this chronological calculation shows very
clearly the new intensity of the idea of the end of time starting
with Bengel's predications. First, the year 1809 was for him the
year of the return of Christ and the beginning of the Kingdom
of a Thousand Years. On the basis of later calculations, he proposed
the year 1846 as the final end. Thus, world history, according
to the plan of divine economy established by his labors, had hardly
more than a century left before it: this brief period had to contain
everything the plan of divine economy still foresaw for man: the
Beast arising from the depths, the abyss, the appearance of the
great tempter, of the Antichrist, the calamities of the end of
time, the violent purification of the Church, the supreme combat
between the Kingdom of God and the Kingdom of Satan on this
earth. Thus, the idea of progress from Enlightenment philosophy
made way here for a dramatic sense of the end of time, considering
history as having already attained its final and decisive stage.
All religious interest passed over to history.

   This tendency is shown in all the impetus of piety characteristic of pietism. From all sides, one watches for the "signs
of the times," one attempts to perceive in the great historical
events the fulfillment of New Testament prophecies, more particularly those of the Apocalypse. Everywhere one senses the Antichrist
and his prophets. At the same time, the image of the "Golden
Age," the realization of the Kingdom of God, the Kingdom of
a Thousand Years, the completion of the final phase of world
history, when the terrible conflicts between the Community of
God and the Antichrist will be overcome, when the Serpent will
be chained in the abyss, and when Christ with his scepter will
feed his flock, appears more and more strongly in the spiritual
considerations of the Community. The apocalyptic feeling of the
beginnings of pietism did not only give birth to a new Christian
interpretation of history, to a new representation of the Last
Judgment, but also to a new chiliasm, strongly preoccupied with
the form the Society finally realized at the end of history, will
have to take. [88]

   The consciousness of the approaching end of time, the
feeling of having arrived at the last era of the history of salvation
culminated in a new attitude to history in general. Hereafter,
all at once, an intuitive glance discovers how many historical
events of the past are conducted according to a hidden and mysteri-

ous plan, and how all things of an apparently contradictory sort are brought together in the vast tableau of the history of salvation. It was necessary for the end to be near in order for the meaning of history to be revealed when, in previous epochs, it had remained buried in the impenetrable clouds of an enigmatic future. Bengel expressed this idea in a simple manner:

> Old people, he said, have a preference for biographies: thus, as the world is beginning to become old it also collects its biographies; that is why historical studies are making such progress. [89]

This combination of eschatology and history will characterize all the philosophy of history of German idealism.

This theological view of history, envisioned as a history of salvation, contains a whole series of idea-forms which will be found later on in the philosophy of history of the idealist thinkers.

1. We are struck first by the great interest given to the division of history into periods. This interest is due to the desire to throw into relief with the greatest possible clarity the different stages of the plan of divine economy. In fact, the old theology already contains the theological pre-requisites for setting history into periods. In Bossuet, history is a triumphant display of the divine majesty, represented here below by the assured triumph of the church.

In Bengel, and in his predecessors of Reformed origin, Jean Coccejus (1603-1669) in particular, and Campegius Vitringa (1659-1722)--especially in his **Panegyricus de regno Dei** (1660), history is a series of alliances between God and the elect saved from the fall. This history of salvation is realized in a spiritual evolution through these alliances, until the final battle between the Kingdom of Light and the Kingdom of Darkness. In Bengel, these suggestions become even stronger as he also wishes to see a chronological conformity between the periods. His book, **Weltalter** (The Ages of the World) [90] a title that one finds again, significantly enough, in Schelling, represents an attempt at a chronological fixation of the divine plan of redemptive history, with the aid of the varied numerical data from Old and New Testament prophetic books.

Here, Bengel devoted himself to downright feats of mathematical jugglery, with the intent of harmonizing the Bible's varied numerical data.

These calculations have no more value for us than that of curiosity. However, the attempt to divide church history and human history into epochs according to the criteria of the inner redemptive economy had to have a decisive effect upon the historical metaphysics of German idealism. Thus, for example, the division of history into three periods, outlined by Schelling in his **System des transcendentalen Idealismus,** is dominated by the fundamental idea of the progressive revelation of God by himself in the course of history. In Schelling, this division into periods also emerges into an eschatology:

> The third period will be when what was presented in the preceding periods in the form of destiny or nature will take the form of providence and will be revealed when what seemed to be only the work of destiny or nature will constitute the beginning of a providence revealing itself imperfectly. When this period will begin, we cannot say; but when this period will be, God will be.

Schelling too, sees in the end of history the fulfillment of the realization of God by himself when "God will be all in all" (I Cor 15:28).

2. In Bengel, the idea of evolution does not coincide with the idea of progress of Enlightenment philosophy. The development of redemptive history does not evolve along a path of rectilinear ascension, but in a dramatic dialectic. The latter is the dialectic of the struggle between God and Satan, which takes place in the world and where man is the stake. From here comes the dramatic character proper to history of the world, which dominates the whole spread of the history of the world. Here again, Bengel took certain themes from theology. Acontius had already described the historical process from the point of view of stratagemata Satanae, Satan's stratagems of war. [91] God would like to bring about his plan of salvation, but Satan opposes him in ever-changing forms and ever-different disguises. Each era has its own forms of Satanic resistance to God's saving work, and in each era God puts into effect new methods of action to unmask and conquer Satan's resistance. Bengel places this dialectic at the base of his whole explanation of the Apocalypse:

> A great malady must be fought and overcome by antagonistic, powerful, saving measures. [92]

He pushed this dialectic so far as to oppose the dogma of the divine Trinity, a dogma of the infernal Trinity, also developed out of The Apocalypse according to Saint John. [93]

This dialectic is not of mythical, but of historical essence: the struggle between the infernal and heavenly trinities becomes real in the course of history, with an ever-increasing violence. The more the Kingdom of God increases, the more energy God puts into his saving work, the stiffer grows the Devil's resistance. And the apocalyptic vision dominates anew. Of his own era, Bengel says: "Evil increases with such vigor that one has difficulty imagining that it could go very much further in its growth." [94]

This is for Bengel a new proof of the accuracy of his conception that the contemporary era constitutes the ultimate one. The dramatic dialectic of the history of salvation precipitates us toward the supreme struggle with frightening speed. In this regard, Bengel refers directly to the words of the Gospel, saying that the Devil "has little time" (Rev 12:12):

> The Devil descended on earth in great anger, for he knows that he has little time. Now, of this little time only a small amount remains, not even a hundred years. How great must his anger be now! Nevertheless, the Kingdom of God continues on its way. [95]

Thus, the idea of progression in the history of salvation must always be understood in relationship to this dialectic. There is no doubt that this relationship of the idea of a progressive revelation of the divine economy and this dialectic provides the theological archetype of the historical metaphysics of German idealism. In Hegel, as well as in Schelling or Franz von Baader, the relationship of the historical dialectic to the idea of evil is maintained.

3. Oetinger developed this idea by endeavoring to establish the strict rules of God's method of providential action, rules which will be found again in the historical metaphysics of German idealism. It is not surprising if the eschatological image Bengel makes of history contains the religious source of certain ideas which appear as characteristic of the Hegelian historical vision in the most restrained sense; in particular the Hegelian idea of "the ruse of reason" (List der Vernunft). Viewed from outside, history is the place of the expansion of the private egotism of individuals and groups. Those with power act as they intend; each one wishes to attain his objective by his own action. But from the moment an act has taken place, the actor ceases to be the master of his actions. The act not only produces the repercussions its instigator desired, but also has boundless and unforeseen consequences, leading to unimaginable and often completely unexpected primary and secondary results. It is there precisely that the absolute spirit's plan of incarnation takes place. The "ruse of reason" consists of making use of man's egotism to give form to sublime, concealed projects and to combine in a higher inspiration the contradictory or apparently senseless acts of individuals. [96]

This idea is contained in a theological interpretation of history in its totality, which sees in every event, in the last analysis, an element of the divine plan of redemption. The idea has already been expressed in simple form by Luther, when he makes the princes and the powerful the marionettes or the "puppets" of God. [97] Already in Luther the following idea dominates: the princes pursue their politics of power and want to carry out their own projects by means of their power. They believe they are acting for themselves, whereas in reality they are only marionettes in the middle of a wider game, which God in person plays with them and by which he fulfills his projects, not theirs. In Bengel's historical theology, so dominated by the idea of a permanent and progressive plan of redemption, Luther's idea returns in a more elaborate form:

> The world has its order of causes and is preoccupied with utility, interest, profit and advantage; but that seems to be only its own desire, and it must also serve the work of Christ . . . so we must likewise learn to consider in this light all forms of government. [98]

Bengel then gives a series of examples taken from the history of the Church.

This same idea appears regularly in Oetinger's historical theology. Thus, he says in his "Golden Age":

> Consequently, God spreads out the remaining peoples of the earth so that they contribute to good on this earth: all the virtues and all the favors of the world, all the evil spirits, all the atheists inspired by the evil spirits, must come together there. [99]

This idea, quite naturally, leads to the fundamental problem of idealistic historical theology, which is that of the relationship between freedom and necessity.

4. This theological and historical concept also includes a relationship between historical research and prophecy. One of the fundamental ideas of German idealism's historical metaphysic is that history and prophecy go together, that historical research is a kind of prophecy in reverse--an apparently fairly arbitrary idea if it is taken out of its original context, the religious order.

In Bengel, this context appears again with perfect clarity: the Christian, who is privy to the secrets of the divine economy, is at the same time historian and prophet. In the prophetic writings of the Old and New Testaments, he discovers the plan for the general unfolding of the history of redemption. A prophetic inspiration shows him what point the divine plan has reached in his own time. Looking back, he has dominion over the different stages and epochs of the divine plan of redemption and the wonderful footprints God has left in the past. Full of astonishment and devotion, he sees how the prophecies of the divine plan of redemption have already been made real there, step by step. But once he attains, in the general ou⁺line of redemptive history, the point which represents the present for him, this makes him not only, facing the past, a historian, but equally, facing the future, a prophet, for the consideration of the prophetic writings, especially the Revelation according to Saint John, reveals to him everything which still has to occur, from the present instant until the end of time, what prophetic events have still to take place before the completion of all things. The relationship between historical research and prophecy consists in the glimpse of the overall plan of the divine economy which is granted to pious intuition.

5. Idealistic philosophy makes God's development emerge in the intellectual vision of the absolute spirit catching hold of the Self. In this intuition, in this "point of view," the true completion of theogony is realized. This "point of view" is realized in the form of a universal science, in which the knowledge of theology, of law, of natural sciences comes together in a central vision. Here, Oetinger shows the relationship of the ideas of Jacob Boehme on the central vision (Zentralschau) and Bengel's historical theology. In Bengel, it is God who becomes real in the history of mankind, step by step, according to a precise providential plan to build his Kingdom. This plan will be effectively completed at the end of history under Christ's command in the Kingdom of a Thousand Years. But, already for Oetinger, God will be finally for us the Alpha and Omega. [100]

Bengel himself is not particularly preoccupied with the state of advancement of the faithful's knowledge in the final kingdom. Oetinger, on the contrary, was much more interested in the question of knowing in detail the form to be taken by the spirituality of the members of the "ideal republic," of the Golden Age. The fundamental spiritualistic element of his expectations for the end of time stands out more clearly in him than in Bengel. This end of time will be characterized by a general pouring out of the Holy Spirit:

> What will occur in the Kingdom will be: 1) the Lord will pour out his spirit onto all flesh . . . 2) the splendor of the Lord will appear in a palpable and visible form in different representations, his gifts of prophecy and all his gifts of knowledge being revealed. [101]

The coming together of these gifts of the spirit occurs in a central vision exalting the faith of the Kingdom's subjects to the level of knowledge, of an intellectual intuition. They will participate in a "central knowledge." The description of this knowledge of the future already constitutes a direct foreshadowing of the idealistic idea of knowledge such as we will find in different forms in Schelling, Hegel, and Baader:

> Theology, Law, and Medicine will form only one knowl-
> edge, the emanation of a single wisdom. Everything will
> be again as it was in the beginning. Our Savior wishes
> to bring about a reform according to the Word. He will
> put in motion the immutable laws of nature . . . Everyone
> will have within himself the simplest basic wisdom and
> understanding of Law, Medicine, and Theology. [102]

Analytic learning will be replaced by intuition. Everyone will
be able to grasp intuitively the meaning of history:

> It will be very easy to understand: God will present
> all things in an intuitive form; and we will see his reckon-
> ings in an architectural vision, in detail and in totality,
> in the physical as in the moral; but above all we will
> have a very sharp knowledge of the history of nations.
> And what the Holy Revelation only outlined, will be re-
> counted in all detail, drawn out of the abyss, set beside
> every kind of state or constitution and seen under the
> righteous enlightenment of the knowledge of God, of
> the soul, and of the human body. There will be no more
> than one single basic wisdom. Jurisprudence and medicine
> will no longer be separable from theology; history will
> be the public theater of God's ways and of all providence,
> of all the phrases of Solomon. . . . It will be the source
> of all knowledge. The law will come from theology,
> and medicine will be no more than an emblematic theology;
> we will see in souls and in bodies the imprint of the
> being from whom all things have come forth . . . [103]

The whole concept of knowledge which will be that of
German idealism is thoroughly foreshadowed here; and no more
than one step is necessary to arrive at the idea that in this intuition
and in this central knowledge of the believers or rather the visionaries of the end of time, God attains a total consciousness of
self. This step is also foreshadowed in Oetinger, in the same terms
which will be later Hegel's:

> The spirit contains all within itself; to a certain degree
> reason exalts the whole to the level of an abstract idea
> and at the time of the Golden Age one will find true
> to the highest degree what is, after so many false defini-
> tions, the true definition of knowledge, the true knowledge.
> The quintessence of divine things, the base of which
> is in the spirit and which then spreads into the reason.
> God buried it in the spirit. The seeker has with God's
> help to take it in to the reason. Reason must be in accord
> with the spirit, and the spirit by the same token must
> be in accord with God. [104]

Thus, the central process of the Hegelian philosophy of identity is described exactly. In reason, the absolute spirit becomes conscious of itself. In Oetinger, this central vision still has its original eschatological character. It is to be found at the opening of the evolution of the history of redemption and could not exist elsewhere. God's expansion in nature and in the history of redemption is necessary for him to attain full consciousness of himself at the end of time:

> God, before the creation of the world, has had the inten-
> tion through Christ to pass from the beginning to the
> end, from the Alpha to the Omega of numerous periods
> or eternities, until man was formed and God was all
> in him. [105]

This small expression "in him" represents the step taken by Oetinger, beyond Bengel, in the direction of the philosophy of identity which is found in Hegel and Schelling.

The central vision of the man of the Golden Age includes, at the same time, God's progressive revelation through himself. Thus, it is clear why in Oetinger the definition of the divine being as the revelation of itself holds central place. "The being of God is in the manifestatio sui, in the revelation of self." [106] God, the supreme being, is seen as a pure and simple manifestation, which Hegel will express in the following manner:

> The definition of the spirit is . . . the manifestation . . .
> His definition and his content are this revelation itself.
> [107]

The great quarrel between Schelling and Hegel, who both saw in God the ens manifestativum sui, was concerned with the precise question of the way in which revelation should be conceived. Hegel had a quite rigid and "deterministic" concept on this point, maintaining that the manifestation of God flows from the very essence of the mind and spirit. Schelling, on the contrary, placed God's liberty at the center and criticized Hegel's attempt to attach the divine essence to a precise law of development:

> It is now a very common idea to see in the whole history
> of the world a progressive revelation of God. But how
> has the divinity arrived there, how has it begun to reveal
> itself? The response: God is by nature and necessity
> a being who reveals himself (ens manifestativum sui),
> is concise, but not exact. [108]

Schelling rejects the necessity of creation and insists on the liberty, the "superabundant," the "boundless liberty" of

God. He writes in **Die Weltalter:**

> Thus, the divine life, like any other life, also has its periods of development. The difference is simply that God is the freest being of all and that the developmental periods of his life depend only on his liberty . . . Each period of divine revelation constitutes a limitation within himself . . . The choice of what is to be revealed and what is to remain hidden depends upon the free will of the mind and spirit, which is at the same time that of the Father of all things. [**109**]

Here, Schelling follows word-for-word an idea of Oetinger, who, on this point, differs from Bengel exactly as Schelling differs from Hegel. Whereas in Bengel, taking into consideration only the schematization of the mathematical calculations of the periods of redemptive history, one has the impression that the unfolding of the divine economy is the realization of a necessity responding to a law situated in God. Oetinger puts more emphasis on the idea of a sovereign, absolute, and unfathomable freedom of God. He does not tire of stressing this sovereign liberty of God, in relationship to the description of the plan of redemptive history. In his idea of God, the image of the creative, sovereign and free artist always predominates:

> God's governance often appears extremely chancy to man. They think God allows everything to drift along as it does for cattle and vermin, who have no God . . . But in reality everything follows God's public law . . . God, who could have created heaven and earth in the most perfect order instantaneously, did not wish to do so; but from total chaos he formed little by little the greatest regularity; and by the fall, he made it tumble again into chaos in order that one might admire his sovereign and independent freedom and goodness constituting the ultimate meaning of his works, and in order that one might not think he wished only to show himself in the light of his wisdom. Such is basically God's supreme public law; his depths contain an eternal liberty. [**110**]

On the basis of a similar concept of redemption, Bengel would appear as a Hegelian, and Oetinger a follower of Schelling.

But the apocalyptic view of history has still another consequence of great importance. It is a permanent trait of historical idealistic metaphysics that its concept of the end of time passes to a new concept of human society. This idea has been expressed--and this was one of the reproaches addressed to Hegel--by saying that in Hegel the State replaces the Kingdom of God. This end of time marked by the attainment of a perfect society comes directly from the theological prototype of this historical thought. According to Hegel, providential evolution comes to an end in Christ's return and the coming of the Kingdom of a Thousand Years. This event, according to his calculations, will reach humanity in less than one hundred years. This relatively brief delay, according to the same calculations, will be essentially occupied by the ordeals and by the evils of the end of time. Thus all his writings are dominated by the general tone of this warning:

> The good is ripe for the harvest, and the evil approaches its autumn; the just will be gathered into the garner of the Lord, and the atheists will be swept away in great number and thrown into the press of wrath . . . We are not far from these great things. Act accordingly. [111]

> Already men are born who will see all these things; but there will be more than one grave situation in this period. [112]

> Our children and our children's children will see great things. [113]

If Bengel was obliged to reveal to his own generation the terrifying prospect of having to live in the period of the last ordeals of the church, the expectancy of the end of time appears to the representatives of the following generation in a new guise, which is described most clearly by F. C. Oetinger. Indeed, this generation, and the following one, were to experience the return of Christ and the beginning of the Kingdom of a Thousand Years. The apocalyptic consideration of history emerges, then, from the time of the disciples of Bengel, by virtue of a logical application of the master's doctrine into a reflection on the state of perfection attained by human society during the "Golden Age."

Eschatological thought outlines a picture of the final state of humanity, by starting from the following point of view: such is the reality which awaits us, to which all the historical evolution of preceding periods leads us, and--decisive point--for which we have to prepare ourselves. This last element introduces into the expectation of the end of time a factor of social and political activity. The final perfect society, for apocalyptic thought, is not an abstract utopia, but a historical reality set in the immediate future; and which must be prepared now through the efforts of the generation living at the present time. [114]

Thus, the expectation of the end of time, set down by Bengel, gives rise in Oetinger to a specific reform of the ethical, social, political, and pedagogical order, the realization of which he expects from the princes and governments of his time. In a certain sense, the picture of the Golden Age sketched by Oetinger provides the mold which will shape the outlines of the ultimate state of society, of the state or the ideal society, such as we will find in Hegel, Schelling, and Baader, but also in Karl Marx; and it is noticeable that not only some of Hegel's important concepts appear in Oetinger's description of the Golden Age, but also some of Marx's. [115]

Here, we find we are in the midst of different and very surprising facts. The most striking characteristic of Oetinger's outline of the "Golden Age,"--he places its beginning in the year 1836--is, without doubt, the idea that the social order of the Golden Age will be democratic. From the idea of the universal priesthood, from the idea that in Christ there is neither free man nor slave, neither Greek nor Roman, Oetinger drew the conclusion that in the Kingdom of God, when the original image of God will be reinstated in man, all men will be equal. It is surprising, therefore, to find that the specifically democratic trait of Swabianism, which appeared particularly in the great democrats of the 19th century such as Uhland and the Swabian politicians of 1848, also finds its roots in the traditions of indigenous pietism. German democratic ideas do not rest solely on the ideology of the French Revolution, but find roots in the Christian conscience of Swabian pietism. Here, from the beginning, Swabian pietism adopted a position all its own, for the Swabian pietistic pastors were the first to fight with vigor and courage, in the name of Christian liberty, the absolutist government incarnate in their absolutist princes of the 17th and 18th centuries.

This Swabian milieu--where resistance to discredited overlords and to the state church was one of the strongly defended articles of the tradition of pietism--was necessary for a theologian such as Oetinger to dare to speak in his work of an imminent suppression of absolutism on this earth and of the restoration of liberty and equality among men under the direction of Christ:

> True happiness, in a kingdom, implies three conditions, first that the subjects, despite the variety which order implies, and despite differences in condition, know among themselves an equality similar to that which is presented to us in the division of the country of Israel, the equality of each plot of ground reminding us that no one must think he is superior to his neighbor. Every man should find his happiness in the happiness of another, his joy in the joy of all others. [116]

Still more astonishing is the declaration in which Oetinger proclaims the progressive suppression of private property in the social order of the "Golden Age." The picture of the "Ideal Republic" of the ideal governments, includes, among other things, the introduction of absolute co-ownership, in which Oetinger sees the second condition for true happiness in a kingdom:

> Secondly, they should possess all goods in community and not get upset about things being their own property. In fact, men possess a great number of things in common, churches, schools, roads and streets, waterways, markets, noble estates, hospitals, etc. By nature, each has the right to use the goods of another as much as the other to use his. [117]

The third condition of true happiness is also of a social nature. It consists of the fact:

> . . . they have no need for any kind of obligation one to another, for if everything were superabundant, there would be no need for government or property, bonds of constraint imposed by power; everyone would be disposed to lend a hand to each other, in case of need, without obligation; everyone would be content to barter and no form of money would be in use. [118]

For Oetinger, the perfect social order of the Golden Age is a re-establishment of Paradise:

> Just as this third condition of happiness subsisted in paradise, whereas its contrary--violence of one against another, owners of property and contracts making use of the work and services of others--appeared after the fall, so, at the time of the Golden Age, equality and power, co-ownership of goods and property without any question, exemption from all servitude and obligation and attachment for work and slavery will be so arranged that, for the very least, community property and freedom from servitude and contracts will be supreme in all things. [119]

The world order, at the time of the Golden Age, will give way to love: When

> . . . the eyes of the subjects will see the king in his beauty (Isa 33:17) . . . the law will no longer serve as power exercised by violence, but as free government by love, not for the usurpation which is single ownership, but for communal sharing, not for imposed servitude, but for the communal operation of the kingdom and mutual aid . . . There will no longer be written law; the secrets of Holy Scripture and the reasoning of the priests will make decisions instead of the civil laws. Consequently, all the causes of vanity of which Solomon speaks will be eliminated; and in all things true happiness will be enjoyed, if not in a paradisical manner, at least in the greatest love. [120]

Here is the program of the French Revolution--liberty, equality, fraternity--set down in the work of a Swabian pietist thirty years before the revolution itself.

The ultimate result of the vision of history in the perspective of the end of time is, then, just as it appears here: the picture of a perfect society resting on equality among all, on fraternity, and on community property. If one considers the direct relationships between social utopia and eschatology, [121] it is easier to understand how it happened that Hegelian eschatology could be turned around to produce Marxist eschatology. If the Christian elements are removed from the image that Oetinger gives of the perfect society of the Golden Age, one would see emerging from Oetinger the ideal society of Communism constituting the final form of historical evolution. Conversely, it is apparent that a great many old religious and messianic elements remain alive in Marx, despite the secularization and the purely materialistic foundations of his social theory.

Chapter Four

THE CABALISTIC SOURCES OF THE ROMANTIC
PHILOSOPHY OF NATURE

Christian cabalism comes from a very ancient tradition. [122] It goes back to the compulsory conversions of the Spanish Jews in the 13th century. Some of these converts tried to justify themselves to themselves and to their friends by discovering in the Jewish cabalistic tradition reflections of the Christian dogmas of the trinity and Christology. Also, Spanish Christian missionaries, like Raymond Lulle, for example, charged with the conversion of their Jewish compatriots strove to demonstrate to the Israelite believers that their religious conviction represented by the cabala already contained the essence of the Christian faith. This tradition of a Christian interpretation was re-established in Renaissance philosophy, by Pico della Mirandola, who was condemned by the Roman Inquisition because of his conviction that no body of knowledge existed which demonstrated the divinity of Christ as well as the cabala. [123]

The German protagonist of a Christian interpretation of the cabala was Reuchlin, [124] the great humanist, professor at the University of Tübingen, teacher of Melanchthon. He published several works on the cabala, **De verbo mirifice** (1494) and **De arte cabbalistica** (1517) and explained that a primordial revelation in the texts of the cabala was fully realized in Jesus Christ. Reuchlin was the founder of an original cabalistic Christian tradition, which was preserved throughout the following centuries, especially in the circles of Swabian theosophical scholars. It appeared strikingly in the person of Princess Antonia of Wurttemberg, herself a follower of a minister-scholar who still held to the tradition of Reuchlin in the middle of the 17th century and introduced her to the mysteries of cabalistic theology. [125] She had a symbolic and emblematic representation of the cabalistic doctrine and the mystical relationships between the Old and New Testaments painted on the walls of a church at Teinach-les-Bains in the Black Forest. This cabalistic picture still exists today. Oetinger re-discovered it and published a now famous book, **Öffentliches Denkmal der Lehrtafel.** [126] In it he developed, with the aid of a detailed interpretation of the symbolic picture, a whole system of Christian theosophy, adopting the principal doctrines of the Christian cabala, especially the doctrine of sefirot, always centered in Christ.

Oetinger was not the only one among the pietists who returned to the cabalistic Christian tradition. The most famous book on this subject was published by a pietist nobleman, Baron Christian Knorr von Rosenroth (1636-1689) [127] entitled **Cabbala denudata**, Vol. I, 1677, Vol. II, 1684. This book made a deep impression on all the great minds of the time--Leibniz, [128] for example--and was read especially by the mystics of radical and separatist pietism in the circles of Frankfurt, Berlebourg, Wittgenstein and Budingen. Oetinger was the mediator of cabalistic ideas for the German idealistic philosophers, especially for Schelling, who returned often to the Swabian theological sources, with which he had been indoctrinated in his youth during his sojourn as a theological student at the Stift, the seminary at Tübingen, and which he called to mind in all the decisive crises of his spiritual and philosophical development. [129]

The doctrine of sefirot speaks of the reflections, the radiance, and the effulgence of God. This doctrine of radiance is nothing more than the attempt to express in a mythological as well as metaphysical way the process of God's manifestation, of his self-revelation, of his manifestatio sui, self-manifestation. If Schelling, in his philosophy of nature, returns to the idea of God as ens manifestativum sui, the being manifesting itself in a permanent act, the being who becomes real by manifesting itself in the plentitude of its creative and formative forces, he does so under the direct influence of Oetinger. [130] Oetinger, for his part, is inspired by Jacob Boehme and by the Christian cabala, which is the source or rather one of the sources of Boehme's theosophical work, with the sole difference that the cabalistic sources of Oetinger are well known, whereas it seems impossible to prove the cabalistic sources, probably oral, of Jacob Boehme. [131]

The basis of this idea of God revealing himself exists in all the cabalistic tradition, the meaning of the name revealed to Moses by the voice speaking in the burning bush (Exod 3:14): "I will be what I will be." The being of God is an unfathomable depth of free-will ready to be revealed, realized, embodied and represented in corporal and visible forms. It is very difficult to express this basic idea in French [or English, (tr.)] because in French [and English] there is only a single word for what is called in German Leib and Kërper. Both words are translated as "body" but Leib is not identical with body, because "body" always expresses a material thing, whereas Leib is a much wider term which comprises visible and invisible forms, spiritual and material realities.

The angels and the spirits have their Leib, their spiritual bodies; they are not abstractions; they have their own Leiblichkeit, and that means more than corporality. [132]

According to Jacob Boehme, the angels' fall was the cause of the contraction of matter which appeared as compact matter only after the angels' revolt. The restoration of the Kingdom of God is understood as the attempt to raise fallen creation into the Kingdom of Light, in a heavenly and spiritual corporality identical with the luminous body of God. According to the secret doctrine of the cabala, repeated by Jacob Boehme and by Oetinger and still once again by Schelling, it is God himself who has a body; and the corporality, die Leiblichkeit, is not foreign to the being of God, but belongs to his perfection and is an element proper to this perfection of his being. "Corporality is the end of the ways of God," says Oetinger; and it is with this same formula, repeated by Schelling, that he expresses the essence of his philosophy of nature. [133]

The doctrine of sefirot describes the process by which God manifests, realizes, and reveals his limitless being, in his diverse radiations or effulgences or reflections, ten in number, according to tradition. Basically, it describes the theogonic process, the theogony understood in the sense that this theogonic process does not consist of an intellectual act in the consciousness of God, but in a successive corporal realization, in a continual incorporation (Verleiblichung). The end would be the total manifestation of the forms and powers hidden in the depths of the divine being, the self realization in full splendor and radiance of his being become manifest, corporal--a spiritual body, a heavenly body.

This process of the self-manifestation of God implies and comprises his manifestation in the universe, in nature as well as in history; it is a process as much creative and preservative as soteriological. The evolution of the universe through the different kingdoms of inorganic matter, plants, animals, and man belongs as much to this theogonic process as to soteriology, which forms a kind of prolongation or continuation of creative evolution in the kingdom of history. Today, when there is an impassioned discussion on the soteriological evolution of Teilhard de Chardin, we must remember that the term evolution was not introduced first by the scholars of 19th century natural sciences around Charles Darwin, but that the term was introduced as a theological and soteriological one by the 18th century theosophists. Thus, it was adopted by the German idealistic philosophers, Hegel, Schelling, Baader, as a soteriological term to describe the theogonic process in which God manifests himself as much in the universe as in soteriology "in order that God may be all in all" (I Cor 15:28). This verse of Saint Paul, which is so often cited by Teilhard de Chardin, is the favorite verse of Schelling, Baader, and before them Oetinger. It was Baader who published an essay on evolution-ism and revolutionism, [134] or positive and negative evolution of life in general and of social life in particular in the **Bayerische Annalen**, Vol. 28, 219-224 and Vol. 62, 483-490.

Saint Martin adopted this doctrine of sefirot in the form found in Jacob Boehme as the idea of the seven forms or bases of God, which, also following Boehme, he calls the seven wheels, the seven spiritual springs and fountains. He explains how Boehme "attempts to give to these seven fundamental qualities names in order to make them understood as he maintains we do not have enough words in our languages, which, according to him, are degraded like man and the universe." [135] He calls them "astringency" or "coercive power," "malice" or "bitterness," "agony," "fire," or the "fiery lightning," the "sound" and finally "the being," "the substance" or "the thing itself." [136] This last form or power is called Leiblichkeit, by Boehme. The actual expression does not appear in Saint-Martin because it did not exist in French at that time. He speaks of "the thing itself" because, he contends, "it is only then that it reveals to us the completion of its existence and the completion of all the powers which preceded." That is precisely what Oetinger expresses with the phrase: Die Leiblichkeit, the being, the celestial body, the thing itself "is the end of the ways of God, which discloses the completion of his existence." [136a] On the other hand, the "completion of the existence of God" is the exact translation of what Schelling calls theogony.

Schelling himself takes this idea of Leiblichkeit, as the basis of his critique of pure idealism. Previously, Oetinger had denounced pure and abstract idealism as "alarm in the face of materialism"; he had already criticized the purely formal and abstract understanding of the spirit, and judged the dualism of Descartes as the unfortunate beginning of the disunion of idealism and materialism expressing itself in the disunion of modern natural sciences and theology. Following him, Schelling himself rose up against a purely idealistic interpretation of being, against the contempt of the physical and against a purely abstract and formal-istic interpretation of the spiritual world. He developed his ideal realism--Ideal-Realismus--as a base for a universal restoration of the lost unity of the knowledge of nature and the spiritual world, of a vision or universal science, which he predicted as the future end of the evolution of the sciences. Schelling returns almost word for word to the definition of Oetinger, of course without mentioning him:

> This divine power comprising the whole does not encom-pass only nature but also the spiritual world and the soul residing above them. Thus, they themselves receive by this reunion a spatial relationship. The old belief in a place, a domicile of the spirits again finds its importance

and its new confirmation. This is the ultimate purpose: that everything will be transformed as far as possible into a visible and corporal form. Corporality is, according to the ancients, the end of the ways of God, who wishes to manifest himself as much in space or in place as in time. [137]

The most surprising evidences of the cabalistic and theosophical tradition coming out of Boehme and Oetinger are found in Schelling, in his philosophy of death. In the thirty-second lecture on the philosophy of revelation, Schelling explains death as "essentification" (essentification). Schelling says:

The death of man, is not a separation but rather an essentification, in which only the accidental perishes; but the essential, that which is properly man, will be preserved, for no man appears in his life exactly as he is. It is only after death that he will be himself. There is the terror of death for one, and the consolation for another. At the same time, the accidental good whose evil here is hidden and the accidental bad whose good here below is hidden will disappear. This essentiality, in which even the physical is preserved, must be a being of supreme reality and, of course a being much more real than our present body, which, because of the reciprocal separation of its parts, is only a compound whole and therefore fragile and corruptible. There are words in all languages to express the first sensation of a thing no longer troubled by any reflection, including the fact that one calls a deceased being 'a spirit' and not 'a soul.' One must imagine, then, the whole man, but in a spiritualized state, to use the terminology of essentiality. [138]

This term, "essentification," was created by Schelling, but borrowed from the theosophical, or rather cabalistic, terminology of Oetinger. In Oetinger's Latin and German works, there is a whole group of concepts formed by the word essence such as "essentialize," "essentify," "essentification," "essentificator," (God understood, of course, as the "essentificator"). Essence, according to Oetinger, is the substance, the being of a thing, not in the idealistic sense of the image but as he says in his biblical dictionary:

God does not mean an 'image' as created image, as it is understood by Schwenkfeld, but as an essence, in which everything is in power and in which everything can develop (become). [139]

Thus, essence does not consist only of form, but also of all the power and possibilities of the realization, of the unfolding and evolution of a thing. Because of that, God, in Oetinger, is several times called the essentiator, the essentificator:

> Jehovah, the "essentiator," in reality composes nothing, but he esentialized and unifies the powers. [140]

This "essentifying" work is realized especially in the soul and occurs there by God's utterance:

> The soul is not matter, for it is of divine origin; it is 'essentialized,' not compounded; but 'essentification' or the 'essentiation' of the soul is accomplished by the divine word derived then diverted to that. [141]

In his Lehrtafel, Oetinger writes on this derivation of the eternal word in the soul:

> This derivation simplifies all that can be understood in any purely material sense. It brings unity into the soul. This unity cannot be combined in a primitive composition of powers, but with an 'essentiation,' that is to say, the powers in the act of generation--in fieri--resist at first, but continue to penetrate, and finish by uniting in, a purely spiritual element. There, the transitory, scattered element is transformed into a stable and concentrated element, in which many powers pass progressively from aversion to unity. [142]

This "essentification" is also described by Oetinger--always in the words of the cabala--as "simplification" and "intensification." Essentiare est ad intensitatem et inexistentiam potentiae redigere. (To essentialize is to bring something to intensity and to the non-existence of power.) [142]

Oetinger himself demonstrated this phenomenon of "essentification," by a chemical experiment which he mentions in almost all his works, he was so impressed by it. One day when he had extracted by a chemical process the oil from dry balm leaves, he was very surprised to discover that on the surface of the water the balm oil formed the shape of the leaves of the living plant. There, for him, was the demonstration of the essence of the plant's spiritual body, of the leaves' essential form, which remains even after the total destruction of the plant's material form. In his **Biblisches Wörterbuch**, he took this experiment as proof of the resurrection, which, according to him, is nothing more than "essentification," the simplification of the essence of man, including his corporal form. He writes:

> There the flesh itself becomes spirit. The spirit is a tissue
> of efficacious powers in which many different things
> are united in one single form and in which the image
> of truth or the true image is manifest. [144]

It is even more astonishing to realize that Schelling, who never
had the opportunity to extract oil of balm by a complicated chemical process, makes use of the history of this oil to demonstrate
his own idea of "essentification." This is proof of Oetinger's direct
influence on his philosophy and especially on his ideo-realistic
concept of nature. In his thirty-second lecture on the philosophy
of revelation, Schelling describes two different theories of death,
the one which understands death as the separation of the soul
and body, and the other for which life and death are only different
types of being, on different planes of existence. Schelling himself
adopted the second idea, since the idea of a separation of body
and soul presupposes that man continues to live only in part and
not as a whole man. On the contrary, the second theory calls
for the whole man, who must be considered permanent in both
forms of existence. He writes:

> This other idea would be better to compare the effect
> of death with the process by which the spirit or the
> essence of a plant is extracted. Thus, one imagines that
> all the power and all the life of a plant pass into the
> oil extracted from it . . . Some followers of the doctrine
> of general regeneration even affirm that the drops of
> oil-of-balm form the shape of the balm leaves again.
> I have not seen that personally, it is true, and I will
> not make a pronouncement on this subject, although
> the similar phenomena that can be observed in etheric
> liquid oils reveal a strange life within, and prove that
> it is not a matter of annihilated life but of spiritualized
> life. Thus, the death of man would not be a separation
> but rather an 'essentification.' [145]

This idea of death as "essentification" belongs to the
whole of Schelling's theogony. In each material thing, there is
a spiritual image as essence, and as a point of simplification and
intensification, and, on the other hand, as the point of departure
for universal evolution. This nucleus pushes toward a higher realization, toward a superior power, toward the Geistleiblichkeit, the
representation in a spiritual form or body or "heavenly body,"
as it is called by Henri Corbin: [146]

> It is self-evident that the general state of nature during
> this process in which the divine life, according to the
> supreme will, would be realized in this outer world, could
> not be a fixed and stationary state, but an eternal 'becom-
> ing,' a permanent evolution. However, this evolution has

> its goal, which is for nature to attain a perfect essence,
> spiritual corporality. But, although nature can attain its
> supreme expansion only in the last state of its evolution,
> it is not in each moment of this last (stage) a corporal
> being, but a being gifted with a spiritual or spiritualized
> body, which, reaching the supreme and totally abandoning
> itself there is transformed into matter but, of course,
> matter which compared to ours is all Spirit and all life.

In Schelling, this idea serves to reveal the ways of the evolution of life in its diverse appearances in the kingdom of nature and in that of the spirits. Matter itself is not dead, but it has as a formative principle, this inner spirit of life, this essence, to which Schelling does not cease to refer us. He considers it as his personal task to cure the philosophy of his time--which exercises an abstract idealism and takes pleasure in condemning all materialism--to cure this philosophy of its pride and to assign to the physical its proper rank in the order of things:

> From the corporal itself, an image or spirit of inner life
> continually rises up and seeks unceasingly to be re-em-
> bodied by an inverse process. [147]

Thus Schelling, under the influence of these theosophical and cabalistic traditions, makes himself the advocate of corporality in the face of the pride of what he calls abstract idealism.

In spite of Schelling's effort to cover up his sources, Oetinger's direct influence on him can be proved by another fact: in his speculations, Schelling often turns to Bible verses which he cites in a free German translation of the Hebrew or Greek text that does not follow the Luther translation obligatory for all Protestant churches in Germany. Its author is Oetinger, who, in this translation, introduces a theosophic interpretation different from orthodox Lutheran theology.

For example, in his **Weltalter,** Schelling writes on a favorite theme, the origin of God's self-manifestation:

> The most profound and the most singular aspect that
> we see in this ineffability (Unaussprechlichkeit) of the
> divine being and the manifest coming in the power, which
> attracts and embraces the being and pushes it back into
> the hidden (das Verborgene). The original text of Scripture
> calls heaven and earth 'the expansion of divine power'
> which alludes to the fact that formerly the entire visible
> universe was affected by this negation and was drawn
> out of it by later evolution. But because of that, the
> universe still finds itself denied; and this original negation
> is still the nursing-mother of the whole visible world. [148]

The text cited is the first verse of Psalm 150; but he does not give us Luther's translation, "Praise the Lord in the fortress of his power," but a direct literal translation of the Hebrew text, "Praise the Lord in the expansion of his power," which corresponds to the French translation of the Bible, "Praise the Lord in his sanctuary, praise him in the open spaces, where his power breaks forth." This is a classical verse from the cabalistic doctrine of sefirot, by which the cabalistic attempt to prove the orthodoxy of their speculation on the effulgence, on the expansion and radiance of divine power. [149]

A little later, Schelling writes:

> The expression that heaven and earth are the 'expansion of divine power' does not refer only to the power of attraction present in nature, but to the unifying power which gathers together the All. But the Eternal can be finite only in itself, only itself can comprehend and circumscribe its own being. Thus, the finality of the world toward the exterior comprises and encloses a perfect infinity toward the interior. The entire universe, stretched out and unfolded in space, is nothing more than the palpitating heart of the divinity, which held by invisible powers, continues to beat in an endless pulsation, in a rhythmic expansion and contraction. [150]

In almost all his theosophical writings Oetinger had based his theories on the contraction and expansion of divine life or of the divine heart, on the first verse of Psalm 150. In his **Biblisches Wörterbuch**, for example, Oetinger cites this verse more than ten times, and always in relation to his speculations on the powers of the expansion and contraction in God, in the divine life. In his article on "Space," he finds in this verse, too, a biblical confirmation for the theory of space proclaimed by Isaac Newton:

> . . . who defines space as sensorium die, as the instrument or organ of God's sensibility, with which he is able not only to see all, but also to feel all that exists and all that happens among the inhabitants of this earth: 'Space is not a vacuum of terrestrial powers, but it is full of divine powers, and for that reason David calls it in Psalm 150 "the space of his power." ' [151]

This same idea is found again in Schelling's **Weltalter**, where he adds in the margin of his manuscript to the lines already cited on God's heart:

> Space is this expansion of the enclosing power which expands from the interior.

56

The same biblical relationship between Schelling and Oetinger is found again in the frequent citation of the sixteenth verse of the seventh chapter of the Letter to the Hebrews, where, in the original Greek text, the author speaks of the indissoluble *Zoe* life--zoe akatálytos. This idea of the indissolubility of life is the basis of Oetinger's theology, which he set forth in his famous work, **Theologia ex idea vitae deducta** [152] a book which, from all evidence, inspired Schelling and contributed much to the formation of his own ideas on the philosophy of nature. In **Weltalter**, he writes:

> We know no other God than the living God; the cohesion of his most spiritual life with a natural life is the miracle of indissoluble life, according to the remarkable words of one of the apostles (Heb 7:16). [153]

Schelling's translation is not taken from Luther any more than was Oetinger's. Luther himself had completely ignored the particular meaning of the Greek word zoe akatálytos and translated simply: "endless life." But Schelling adopted the translation of Oetinger, who for his part reproached Luther for not having translated the Greek text well in this case; and for whom the idea of the "indissoluble life" was the basis of his own theology of life, or, according to his expression, "theology deduced from the idea of life." Thus he says in his **Biblisches Wörterbuch**:

> It is written in the Letter to the Hebrews (7:16) that the priest Christ is not installed according to the law of a carnal commandment, but according to the power of an indissoluble life. In conclusion, it is evident that:
>
> 1. In all life there is a bond between different powers;
> 2. that the powers cannot be separated in God himself;
> 3. that God cannot transfer his indissolubility of powers to any creature, since it belongs to God alone;
> 4. that the powers are divisible in the inner creature by misuse of liberty, but not from outside;
> 5. that in this separability or divisibility of powers there is the cause of a possible fall. [154]

All the elements mentioned up to this point are to be found in Oetinger, in their original cabalistic relationship, that is to say, in the detailed interpretations of different sefirot, as established in the work **Lehrtafel**. [155] The series of sefirot begins with the so-called "crown," which is the origin and the source of God's self-manifestation. Oetinger writes of it:

> Through the first sefira, God emerges from his depths as a crown or an immeasurable periphery of the expansion of his innermost point (his sanctuary) (Ps. 150:1) or of his point of concentration out toward his self-manifestation.

The second sefira is the cochma, the "divine sofia," the "virgin sofia," the divine wisdom; and there Oetinger takes up Jacob Boehme's sophiology in all its detail. [156] From this second sefira, bursts forth or radiates the third bina in which the original ideas of the divine consciousness move forward and begin to "play" before God.

The fourth power is gedulah, the stage of God's self-manifestation, in which "God expands his powers in himself" (Ps. 150:1: "Praise the Lord in the expansion of his power"). [157] In Oetinger's Lehrtafel this verse is often used to show the biblical content of the idea of space developed by Isaac Newton. Oetinger continues:

1. God is present in his essence from within and from without;
2. God is present in and through the central powers;
3. These powers extend into infinite space (Ps. 150:4);
4. This space is the sensorium dei (Ps. 150);
5. This space is empty of matter but full of spirit (Ps. 150);

   . . .

15. In eternal space God is all in all. [158]

This "expansion of power" implies the manifestation of God not only in the created being, but also toward the created being and for the created being:

It is true that God lives in himself in his own depths (Urgrund), but he cannot manifest himself the created being in this manner. Thus God can never be seen outside the expansion of his powers, outside his element, outside the spiritual center of his movement within the element. He is God and Father of glory and splendor, who engenders his own glory according to his will. In this glory, God is not without space, not without time, not without self-movement, passivity, or receptivity; he is not without radiance, splendor, or circulation of powers; in sum: all that the created being possesses of qualities of structure, of figuration, of transformation in his body, all that to the nth degree God has in his spirit. [159]

The most precise explanation of this verse is expressed in the following words:

The (glory of God) is not God himself (is not identical with God himself) but the light in which he lives and which is called rakia uesso, the expansion of his power. The victorious powers, the lights, the radiations, the invisible things, the invisibilities of God, the eternal power,

and, according to Job 11:6, the obscurities of God are
included there. This 'power of expansion' is passive and
takes all the forms (Gestalt) given to it by the active
principle, that is to say, the eternal Word, by the central
powers, which are the origin of circular movement. [160]

In the fifth stage of self-manifestation, in the fifth sefira,
God assembles his powers in order that we might praise him in
these very powers, in his gebhurot, as it is written in Psalm 150:1.
[161]

In this stage of the evolution, God, by means of expansion
and contraction, becomes conscious of his own plentitude by the
struggle of ideas and definite forms, which begin to become real
separately.

I cannot continue the enumeration of the other stages
of this theogonic process, and I will limit myself to mentioning
the tenth. Here, God emerges from the act of radiance and enters
into the serenity of the fullness completely revealed and realized
in his everlasting form (ewige Gestalt), on his Sabbath, in his
radiant glory, in the plentitude of his light, in his body of light,
in his kingdom. It is then that God's self-manifestation has reached
total embodiment, that God reveals himself in a spiritual corporality, for "corporality is not lack of perfection; it is perfection
itself." [162]

We find the cabalistic roots of Oetinger's theosophy,
but proceeding from an already Christianized and baptized cabala.
In the wake of Knorr von Rosenroth, Oetinger considered the
cabalistic doctrine of sefirot as the most illuminating way to
clarify more intimately and more distinctly the mystery of the
trinity as expressed in the formulae of the central Christian dogma.
The doctrine of sefirot appeared to him to provide the clearest
illumination of this dogma, which contains not only an interpretation
of the inner life and the movements and inner relationships of
the divine consciousness, but also an interpretation of the theogony,
of the act and progress of the outer manifestation of God by
the proliferation of his powers and forms in the created universe
and in the soul of the man contemplating this universe under
divine light.

Thus, we penetrate the innermost sources of Schelling's
philosophy of nature and the sources of a metaphysical concept
which has gone beyond rationalistic and materialistic philosophy
to an idealistic interpretation of being and also overcome the
danger of an abstract idealism and produced the concept of a
universal science bringing together within itself all the separated
parts of the natural sciences and sacred and profane philosophy:
this was the goal of all Schelling's speculative endeavor and the
spiritual conception of his creative thought. [163]

Chapter Five

THE PLACE OF LOUIS CLAUDE DE SAINT-MARTIN
IN ROMANTIC PHILOSOPHY

1/18

Louis Claude de Saint-Martin was born on January 18, 1743, in Amboise, into a noble and pious family. He studied law, but soon started on a military career, less for love of the business of war than to profit from the leisure time it allowed him for his literary and philosophical studies. This was in pre-Napoleonic times, when, in the army, the ratio between the hours of service and free time was still in favor of free time. In 1768, he had an encounter which was decisive for his intellectual and spiritual development, he met Martinez de Pasqually. This mystery man had appeared all of a sudden from out of the different rival lodges of freemasonry. Martinez de Pasqually's origin remains hidden in shadows he himself did nothing to dispel. It was supposed that he belonged to the cabalistic tradition; it was suggested that he was a Jew of Portuguese origin, but this suggestion cannot be supported by the facts. Probably he was born a good Catholic, in Grenoble. In 1754, he founded the freemasonry rite of Elus-Coens, a branch of the so-called Scottish Rite. The particular characteristic of this lodge was its somewhat aristocratic tendency. Thus, it displayed none of the bourgeois and rationalistic tendencies of English freemasonry, which propagated ideas of equality and fraternity. The other difference was the introduction of new degrees, which revealed mysterious symbols connected with the legend of the assassination of Hiram, the architect of the Temple of Solomon. But the most striking thing about this new branch of freemasonry was the introduction of theosophy, occultism, and alchemy into the lodges. [164]

Martinez de Pasqually appeared in 1760 at Toulouse, later and with more success at Bordeaux, and in 1766 at Paris, where he founded the "Sovereign Tribunal," the supreme authority for the lodges of his rite. He succeeded in gaining many followers throughout France; and in 1768, among others, the young Lieutenant Saint-Martin. One of his most active, but also one of his most headstrong, adherents was Willermoz, the great merchant and freemason of Lyons.

59

I cannot go into the rites of the order of the Elus-Coëns in detail; I will limit myself to describing the principal idea of Pasqually's theosophy, which left its mark on all of Saint-Martin's philosophical and religious ideas. Pasqually believed he was the messenger and charge d'affaires for the superior powers, which, according to him, served as mediators of the divine will. On the subject of his own vocation, he said:

> I am only a feeble instrument whom, unworthy as I am, God wishes to use to remind men, like myself, of their first state of masonry, which means spiritually man or soul, in order to show them that they are really 'God-men,' being created in the image and semblance of this Almighty Being. [165]

Here is the idea of the God-man, which fascinated young Saint-Martin: man understood as minister and fellow-worker of the divine will, charged with the soteriological mission to restore humanity to the perfection of his original destiny, which is to become the image of God. This is the main idea we will find in his work, **Le ministère de l'homme-esprit.**

The goal of becoming divine is even found in his conversations with colleagues in his regiment. Saint-Martin writes (**Posth. Wk.,** I, p. 72, No. 576):

> D . . . an officer in the Brittany regiment, called me one day a spiritualist as opposed to a naturalist which his successes in magnetism would probably have made him prefer. In spite of his agreeable nature and his heroic attributes, he does not realize that it is not enough for me to be a spiritualist; and if he really knew me, he would call me a 'divinist' for that is my true name. [166]

Under the influence of Martinez de Pasqually, Saint-Martin resigned from the army in 1771 and lived in the company of Martinists such as Count d'Hauterive, the abbot Fournié, and J. N. Willermoz, mostly in Paris and in Lyons. At Lyons, he wrote his first work **Des erreurs et de la vérité**, Edinburgh (Lyons), 1775. In it he develops his system of theosophy which appears as his own interpretation of Pasqually's ideas, and which comprises a whole philosophy of nature, of the state, and of society and a theory of knowledge as well as a philosophy of the sciences:

> It was at Lyons that I wrote the book **Des erreurs et de la vérité.** I wrote it for want of something to do and in anger at the philosophers. I was shocked to read in Boulanger that religions were born only in the terror occasioned by natural catastrophies. I composed this work about the year 1774, in four months time and in front

of the kitchen fire, not having a chamber where I could
warm myself. One day the pot of soup even upset on
me and burned me quite badly.

In 1782, he published his second work, **Tableau naturel
des rapports qui existent entre Dieu, l'homme et l'univers.**

It was in Paris, partly at the home of M. de Lusignan,
in the Luxembourg, partly at the home of M. de la Croiy,
that I wrote the **Tableau naturel** at the instigation of
several friends. [167]

This book offered his theosophical ideas in a much clearer
and more profound form with more insight and in a more elegant
style. [168]

During the years that followed he found sustenance in
a theosophical system much more developed and closer to the
Christian tradition than that of his first teacher, Pasqually, or
rather, that of Jacob Boehme. I have already cited his opinion
of Boehme. [169] I will add one more comment from among a
hundred similar ones scattered throughout his works:

My works, particularly the first, have been the result
of my deep concern for the man, and at the same time
reflect the little knowledge I had of the wretchedness
of his existence and the slightness of the impression
that truth made upon him in the state of gloom and
disinterestedness in which he allowed himself to stagnate.
It is, indeed, a lamentable thing to see the little fruit
that he reaped from all that was offered to him for
his advancement. It is not my own works which make
me most bewail this lack of concern; it is those of a
man whose shoe laces I am not worthy to untie, my
dearest Boehme. The man must have turned to stone
or become as the devil incarnate at not having profited
more than he did from the treasure given to the world
190 years ago. [170]

Saint-Martin was introduced to the German mystical
tradition in a very strange way. In general, German mysticism
was little known in France, and that is quite understandable because
there were many French mystics in France who were producing
a fascinating body of literature, such as the works of Madame
Guyon, Madame de Bourignon, and Pierre Poiret. Thus, to all
outward appearances, it seemed superfluous to import mystical
books written in a little-known and hardly comprehensible language.

It was during his long stay in Alsace for three years
that Saint-Martin encountered German mysticism. At Strasburg,

62

he became acquainted with a whole series of extraordinary persons, among others, the Swedish baron Silferhielm, [171] the nephew of the great Swedish visionary Emmanuel Swedenborg, who gave him the most fascinating information about his uncle and who stimulated him to write his book **Le nouvel homme,** under the direct influence of Swedenborg's ideas. It was at Strasburg that he also became acquainted with Jacob Boehme's work. [172] It was in this state of mind, excited by his new discoveries of mystical literature, that he received the first letter from a Swiss theosophist, the Bernese Kirchberger von Liebisdorf, born in 1739, who became his friend and his dearest disciple for the rest of his life. Kirchberger was the first to recommend to Saint-Martin Madame Guyon's works which were still unknown to him; and in his letters he emphasizes the remarkable similarity between Madame Guyon's ideas and those of Boehme. But Saint-Martin came to the opinion that the feminine inspiration of Madame Guyon could not be compared to the masculine inspiration of Jacob Boehme, and that when a man once understood Boehme he could only be satisfied by him. After this correspondence on the subject of the superiority of male over female inspiration, Kirchberger said his good-byes to his former inspirer of the gentler sex and devoted himself totally to Boehme's writings, as expressed and explained by his friend, Saint-Martin. [173]

Once initiated into Boehme, he discovered there was at Berne an old retired pastor, a disciple of Jacob Boehme for forty-three years, who was quite familiar with the three regions of the archangels Michael, Lucifer, and Uriel before and after the first fall of the rebellious angels. [174]

The friendship between Saint-Martin and Kirchberger, brought together by Boehme's theosophy, continued to deepen. This friendship was extended, moreover, to all the mystical and theosophical writers of the great school of Jacob Boehme in Germany, in England, and in the Netherlands, and included even their 16th century predecessors. Since Saint-Martin was French and Catholic, whereas Boehme's theosophy had spread more through the Germanic Protestant countries, Kirchberger was the happy initiator and mediator who introduced his French friend to the works of the English Philadelphians such as Jane Leade, Pordage, and Bromley and familiarized him with the spiritualists among Boehme's disciples such as Friedrich Gichtel, with the theosophists and spiritualists of Berlebourg, such as Hector de Marsay, a French Huguenot emigrant, and even with the works of Protestant spiritualists of the Reformation such as Schwenkfeld and Valentin Weigel. [175]

Of these spiritualists of Jacob Boehme's school, Friedrich Gichtel had the most notable influence on Saint-Martin. Gichtel was the practicing theosophist of Boehme's followers; he had visions of the Virgin Sophia, he had bitter struggles with spirits and demons and was much preoccupied with contributing personally, by his spiritual efforts, to the redemption of the Devil himself. The study of his principal work, **Practical Theosophy**, was a moving experience for the two friends who, in their letters, showed their enthusiasm for "our General Gichtel," as they called this peaceable visionary, the founder of the Order of Angelic Brothers, who was never a general of anything. [176]

Kirchberger was at the same time a friend of Baron von Eckartshausen, in Munich, another well-known German theosophist, author of **The Cloud upon the Sanctuary** . . . [177] Saint-Martin was delighted to encounter a taste for the same kind of speculation in a German theosophist. This same Kirchberger also tried to establish personal contact between Saint-Martin and Jung-Stilling, famous author of **Heimweh** (home-sickness) the great lay writer of the Protestant revival in Germany--the Jung-Stilling who lived at Marburg, where he taught scientific economics at the university, and whose house still has preserved on its door to this day the inscription taken from his principal work, **Das Heimweh:**

> Selig sind die da Heimweh haben denn sie werden nach Hause kommen. [178] (Happy are those who suffer nostalgia for the celestial fatherland, for they will return home.)

The correspondence between Saint-Martin and Kirchberger is particularly concerned with discussing the works of German spiritualists of all ages. It is very important to establish this fact, since it is the first time that this ample tradition of a spiritualist Christianity of the theosophical type, developed within the radical circles of German Protestantism from Valentin Weigel and Schwenkfeld to Jacob Boehme, Gichtel and the hermits of Berlebourg, penetrated into French philosophy. To understand better the particular aspect of Saint-Martin's theosophy and the spontaneous welcome given to his work in Germany, especially in the spiritualist circles of the Protestant and Catholic revival, we must remember these fruits of his friendship with Kirchberger. Even after Kirchberger's death in 1798, he remained one of the vivid sources of Saint-Martin's inspiration.

Oddly enough, in Kirchberger's correspondence with Saint-Martin, the name of his future adversary in Germany is already mentioned, the famous rationalist Friedrich Nicolai of Berlin. In a letter of June 1, 1795, Kirchberger confides to Saint-Martin information about a heinous movement in Germany and in German Switzerland. A secret, quite widespread organization of nonbelievers had been formed with the goal of totally eradicating the Christian religion. The leader of this diabolical band is Friedrich Nicolai of Berlin, his means of action are the secret societies such as

64

"The Illumined Ones." They infiltrate all areas of political life, science, literature and even the church. This is why it is necessary to establish a counter-organization of Christian thinkers to fight this diabolical army of atheism. That is the great theme of the Protestant revival, which we find in the letters of Kirchberger. It is time to make up one's mind; the Antichrist is near or perhaps already born: the good strive to close ranks, as the evil ones have already done. It is necessary to work with all one's might to reconstruct the Temple of God throughout all the lands in these last days, and Saint-Martin finds himself charged by his friend to erect a number of pillars in France. [179]

We will return to this eschatological interpretation of rationalist and atheist philosophy, as expressed in the correspondence, when we speak of the interpretation of the personality and philosophy of Saint-Martin by his adherents and German translators and even by his adversaries in Germany, represented by Friedrich Nicolai, who will condemn him as the protagonist of a crypto-Jesuit obscurantism directed against the torch-bearers of Enlightenment philosophy.

If Saint-Martin was not in personal contact with the German writers and poets of his era, he was at least in contact with the central institution of the German philosophical and scientific life of his times, the Academy of Arts and Sciences in Berlin, founded in 1700 by Leibniz. This academy counted among its presidents d'Alembert and Condorcet, as well as a great number of French scholars among its members. It maintained French traditions, even in the language of its lectures, which was always French. [180] In 1784, Saint-Martin participated in the meetings of the Academy in Berlin. In those days, the academies were still very optimistic; they were convinced that it would be possible to solve the most difficult problems of political, social, and moral life by means of philosophical contests. In 1784 the question posed by the Academy of Berlin was: "What is the best way to bring nations, both primitive and civilized, which have surrendered to all kinds of error and superstitions, back to reason?" [181] Saint Martin wrote on the theme of his contribution:

> This question had struck me enough to make me deal
> with it; but I was far from claiming the crown, since
> I proved the opposite to the Academy: that the question
> was insoluble by human means alone. M. Ferney, the
> Secretary of the Academy of Berlin, showed he agreed
> with me in a letter he wrote to me. Indeed, not only
> was I not crowned, but no one was crowned at the
> first meeting. Thus, the Academy postponed the prize
> to the following year, 1785. But I believed I had said
> all that I had to say, and I did not compete again. It
> was M. Avillon, Pastor of the French Church of Berlin,

> who carried off the prize. But as he took his ideas and solutions from books, and notably from Plato, I do not envy him his triumph. [**182**]

Perhaps, in our present situation, it would be fitting to publish the two contributions.

Although the difference between primitive and civilized nations is officially abolished, the problem of bringing the nations back to reason still exists. It is very important to see that Saint-Martin no longer accepts the basis of traditional rationalism, presupposed, without doubt, by the Academy itself. He no longer accepts reason in the manner of the Encyclopedists as the basis of morality, but begins with a criticism of reason itself. He says:

> If, in the most exact sense, reason is nothing other than an ordinary and practical knowledge of truth, it is difficult to propose a more profound question, and one whose solution might be more useful to the human race.
>
> Indeed, to what happiness could we not aspire, if superstitions were banished from the mind of man and if the ensuing fantasy and cruelty were driven out from his heart. A law reasoned and directed toward good of all kinds would replace these lawless practices which debase and mislead him; his sorrowful time here would be transformed into a delightful sojourn from which order and light would never disappear . . . But as much as this hope should urge us on, so the question which incites us humiliates us when we try to resolve it. For, before responding to the learned tribunal which interrogates us on the methods of transmitting truth to our fellowmen, it is essential to ask ourselves if we ourselves possess that truth; and it is here that we will have less to congratulate ourselves on than to lament.
>
> Let us leave aside the enthusiasm which orators and scholars cause in us by the pompous exposé of supposed riches, and examine with them the diverse orders of knowledge which can be the object of our study; we will soon discover that these seducing artists are more concerned with the colors of their pictures than the correctness of the design. [**183**]

We recognize here the principal theme of his work **Des erreurs et de la vérité**, in which he does nothing more than "examine the diverse orders of knowledge," to discover that "it would necessitate a superhuman and divine enlightenment to reveal the truth to us and to permit us to transmit it to our fellowmen."

It is very understandable that after such a critique of

66

the principal base of contemporary rationalism, the first attack
to be leveled against Saint-Martin after the publication of a German
translation of his works, would come from a group of rationalists
centered in Berlin and who expressed themselves particularly
in the philosophical journals of that city.

Saint-Martin was inclined to have a much more favorable
opinion of German literature and philosophy than his French contemporaries. There is, among his thoughts published in his posthumous works, a chapter entitled "littérature allemande," which
merits being cited word for word because it contains the first
comparison of the philosophical evolution in France and in Germany.
We would emphasize that the following words were written by
a Frenchman, before German idealistic philosophy had begun to
be known in France:

> The Germans think more profoundly than the French.
> The French write more clearly and in a more attractive
> and ordered way. German books are more expensive
> than ours; ours are better made. Also, when we produce
> something of note, the Germans take the form which
> they then apply to their own foundation and reunite
> form and foundation. They are not yet as advanced as
> we are in perverse materialistic philosophy; and the proof
> of that is that they still have systems, while we no longer
> have any--that is to say, we no longer believe in anything,
> because even one system supposes a belief.

> We must not think that the Germans will remain long
> at this point. They are on the way to going further: They
> have already reached the philosophy of Aristotle, and
> God knows where this scholar may lead them. Pythagoras
> had wisdom in head and heart; Socrates had it more
> in heart than in head; Plato had it more in head than
> in heart; Aristotle had it at the tip of his tongue; Alexander
> had it sometimes at the point of his sword, sometimes
> in his stomach; I do not know what place the Germans
> will give it and whether in the long run they will not
> allow it to evaporate completely as we French. [184]

Schickedanz, the translator of these posthumous words,
adds a critical note to this somewhat nihilistic statement:

> This fear of Saint-Martin, quite understandable during
> the era of eclectic philosophy around 1780, was revealed
> as fruitless, because German philosophy underwent change
> for the better through Schelling, Hegel, and Baader.

Among the Germans, two writers visibly influenced Saint-
Martin's thought, Klopstock of Hamburg and Lavater of Zurich.

Saint-Martin was one of several French writers of his era who made use of Klopstock's works. He spoke of him in his posthumous works at the same time as of Edward Young, the English romantic writer, the poet of night and melancholy, who had excited the admiration of Klopstock by his **Night Thoughts on Life, Death, and Immortality** (1742-1745), a book which appeared in many editions and translations in Germany. Saint-Martin wrote of these two thinkers:

> I have often been struck by admiration when reading Young and Klopstock; I have been astonished to see what resource these two writers had found in their own genius to suffice for the plans that they had made for themselves, but I recognize at the same time that if they had been more informed on the lands they traveled through, they would not have made up for the profound truths of which they were ignorant by poetical and literary ornaments. One single passage of our prophets erases all the marvels of their pens. [**186**]

The interesting point of this judgment is that Saint-Martin accepts Klopstock as a poet but does not accept him as a prophet, whereas Klopstock saw himself as religiously inspired, as <u>vates</u> and prophet. Saint-Martin reserved this title for "our prophets," that is to say, for Pasqually and especially for Jacob Boehme. This critical attitude of Saint-Martin is all the more surprising, as Klopstock had the courage to propose an interpretation of the French Revolution completely different from what the majority of his contemporaries gave, particularly the adherents of the Protestant Revival.

This was also an eschatological vision of the revolution but in a completely positive sense. Klopstock is close to glorifying the States-General of France "just as old Simeon glorified the birth of Christ as the date of salvation," and to seeing in the Revolution the "French creation" par excellence in the messianic splendor of the new land under a new sky, in opposition to Lavater and Jung-Stilling, who considered the Revolution as the eschatological revelation of the Antichrist. [**188**] In one of his Odes, Klopstock describes to us the appearance of this "new land":

> As in the twentieth chapter of The Apocalypse According to Saint John an angel descends from heaven with the key of the bottomless pit and a great chain in his hand, and lays hold on the dragon, the ancient serpent, which is the Devil and Satan, and binds him up for one thousand years and throws him into the bottomless pit so that he should deceive the nations no more, thus in Gaul the goddess Liberty will enchain the most terrible of all monsters--war. [**189**]

The joy that the success of the French Revolution excited in Klopstock shows all the signs of a religious exaltation.

Incidentally, Lavater is the only representative of German literature from whom a positive judgment on Saint-Martin's work came to the latter's knowledge, while the other impassioned debates on his works in Germany seem to have escaped him. He writes about Lavater:

> Lavater, a minister at Zurich, is one of those who have most appreciated **L'Homme de désir.** He reviewed it most favorably in his Journal allemand for the month of December 1790. He openly confesses that he did not understand it all; but in truth, Lavater could have understood it all, if he had had the guides. But in the absence of these aids, he remained in the kingdom of his own virtues, which is perhaps more beautiful and more admirable than that of knowledge. And besides, what he had of knowledge he has somewhat 'prodigalized' in his books. Perhaps I should address a similar reproach to myself? This worthy man I do not know personally. [190]

We know that Lavater's friend Sarasin had already given an enthusiastic description of the book **Des erreurs et de la vérité** to his friend and had called Claudius' translation "indescribably sweet and beautiful, especially when read at night and in moonlight." [191] This judgment is not as strange as it seems to us today. There is a whole literature in this era of awakening and romanticism which one could describe as "literature to read in the light of the moon": for example, the **Night Thoughts** of Edward Young; **Der Wolke vor dem Heiligthume,** by Eckhartshausen; and all the nocturnal poetry of the German romantic poets, such as the **Hymnen an die Nacht,** by Novalis.

Lavater, for his part, wrote about Saint-Martin:

> I find few men like him. But until the moment when God himself instructs me otherwise, I must say: Whatever he claims to have, he does not have the simple Christ of the Gospels, for whom I wish to substitute nothing. The Christ of the Gospels is less pretentious and more psychological--the spiritual is not the first element; it is nature first, and then the spiritual--that is the philosophy of Saint Paul and also mine and certainly also that of Christ. The mystification of this man with his 'source of light' is not according to my taste, that is to say, according to the ancient apostolic taste. [192]

We see that later Lavater took a more reserved position in regard to Saint-Martin; his criticism expresses very clearly the general position of a Reformed Swiss pastor and minister who always returns to the simplicity of the Gospel. In the letter to Sarasin mentioned, Lavater also reproaches Saint-Martin for not citing any authority and not presenting any justification for his conceptions:

> The apostles reasoned and gave proofs; they named their authority and took strength from the power of this authority. The mystification of Saint-Martin, who speaks of his 'source of illumination,' is not in the apostolic tradition.

We do not find moderate judgments of this type in Germany. The contrasts there are more defined; there is a tendency either to accept the mystical ideas of Saint-Martin with enthusiasm, to identify with them and to become exalted by his conceptions, or to condemn him violently, as we shall see.

Lavater himself did not know Saint-Martin personally. Of all the contemporary German philosophers and poets, Friedrich H. Jacobi was the only one who had the good fortune--according to him--to be personally acquainted with Saint-Martin in Paris. He speaks of him in a letter to Jean Paul Richter. After having rejected the ideas of Bode and Nicolai about Saint-Martin, which we will discuss later, he continues:

> I have now made the acquaintance of the writer himself in Paris. The chapters on liberty in his book **Les rapports entre Dieu, l'homme et l'univers,** his **Lettre sur la révolution française,** his **Eclair,** his **Ecce Homo,** and the introduction to his work on **L'esprit des choses** have revealed him to me as a remarkable man and writer. Since he lives a very solitary life, as he is held in contempt by all the scholars, theologians, wits and men of the world in Paris, and since I did not want to seek him out at his lodgings, (which were very difficult to find), I succeeded in reaching him only a few weeks before my departure. Afterwards, I spoke with him four times in all and each time for several hours. He holds up remarkably well in philosophical discussions, and he is always happy, full of spirit and good humor. When it was time to say goodbye, he said to me: 'Everybody had told you that I was mad; you have seen that at least I am impudent enough to be happy in my madness. Furthermore, I think that if there are madmen who should be tied up, there are also some to be left free and I count myself among the latter.' [193]

Jacobi continues in his letter:

> He is exactly my age and began only about ten years

ago to learn German with the sole intention of reading
Jacob Boehme, whom he translated into French and takes
for the master-mind among philosophers. Certainly you
know that the school or the sect of Martinists does not
take its name from this Saint-Martin but from a certain
Martinez Pasqualis. Among the Martinists, Saint-Martin
plays somewhat the role of Moses Mendelsohn among
the Jews; the situation of the two is very similar.

Here is the response of Jean Paul to Jacobi:

Thank you very much for your information on Saint-Martin.
I willingly retract what I said of him. [194]

Saint-Martin was first introduced in Germany through
freemasonry. German freemasonry differed from French freemasonry
in its religious rather than political character. Its traditions were
founded in theosophy, in Rosicrucian theories, in alchemy, in spiritism and in spiritualism; there are even some pietistic influences
coming from the Schwenkfeld tradition. [195] In the radical separatist circles of the 16th century, the rationalist and materialistic
philosophy of France had not been admitted. In its political attitude
German freemasonry was conservative and even reactionary in
its defense of monarchical absolutism. We must remember that
the fierce reaction against the completely liberal program of
religious statecraft of the King of Prussia, Frederick the Great,
friend of Voltaire, was the work of Wöllner, who set himself at
the head of German freemasonry and inaugurated under King
Frederick William II, by the edict which bore the name of Wöllner
as responsible minister, an era of the most fierce reaction against
the liberal institutions introduced during the reign of King Frederick
the Great. [196]

However, German freemasonry itself did not totally accept
this reactionary and pietistic spirit. There were liberal circles
which sought to extricate themselves from a theosophy a little
too whimsical for their taste, from a pietism a little too exaggerated, and from a spiritism a little too excessive. These liberals
were partisans of a return to a simple and reasonable program
of reform.

Thus, the Order of the Freemasons of Strict Observance,
which had built on the legends of the Temple and Templars a
whole system of esoteric, spiritistic, and theosophical doctrines,
considered as secret ancient traditions, was exposed to the vehement
attacks of another secret order, the Order of the Illumined (Il-
luminaten-Orden), founded in 1776 in Bavaria. [197] Its founder
was Adam Weishaupt, professor of law at the University of Ingolstadt, fierce adversary of the Jesuits, who were the heads of
the University of Ingolstadt until the suppression of their order

in 1773. Weishaupt, protagonist of a rational morality, propagated his ideas in the German freemasonry circles by assigning as the goal of his movement progress in moral perfection and human happiness. At the same time as rationalism, he introduced anti-clericalism and especially anti-Jesuit mania into the circles of the Illumined. [198]

Weishaupt succeeded in winning over to his ideas the well-known Baron Adolf von Knigge, [199] author of the famous book on the **Umgang mit Menschen,** (Rules of Good Conduct to Observe in Society). Up to that time Baron von Knigge had been an adherent of the Strict Observance. Now Weishaupt used him in his attacks against the Jesuits and against the Rosicrucian brothers. During the years 1781 and 1782, the Illumined very quickly attained an astonishing influence in freemasonry circles in Germany and Austria. The order was exposed to the danger of a definitive split into two rival groups, the one fideistic, the other rationalist and anticlerical.

At this time, Duke Frederic of Brunswick, head of the Strict Observance, attempted to overcome the crisis by the convocation of a great assembly of freemasons of all factions, at Wilhelmsbad. In this way, he thought he could rule on the actual controversies and reestablish a common base of order. The famous Congress of Wilhelmsbad was opened on July 15, 1792.

It was at this critical moment that Saint-Martin entered upon the scene, not in person, but as the author of books distributed to the members of this congress. The conservative wing of the Strict Observance was directed by Willermoz, a friend of Saint-Martin, like him a disciple of Martinez de Pasqually. Willermoz proposed to introduce the philosophy of his friend Saint-Martin as the basis of the religious and philosophical orientation of free-masonry and had already systematically distributed the first work of Saint-Martin, **Sur l'Erreur et sur la Vérité,** among the free-masonry circles in France. [200] In this way he contributed much to the spread of Saint-Martin's ideas first in France, then in Germany and Russia. On the occasion of the Congress of Wilhelmsbad, a Masonic brother brought a whole load of books, copies of Saint-Martin's **Tableau naturel,** which had just been published, and distributed them to the members of the Congress.

This direct manner of <u>Kulturpropaganda</u> had both favorable and unfavorable results for the absent and still-unknown author of these books.

On the one hand, this free distribution contributed enormously to the circulation of his books and ideas in Germany. The great series of German translations of Saint-Martin's books is only the direct consequence of this action, which will be repeated by another German theosopher, the physician and theosopher Obereit von Lindau, who some years later undertook to found his own theosophical order on the basis of Saint-Martin's writings. He also distributed them among persons he wished to join his order. [201]

On the other hand, Saint-Martin was brought into the internal quarrels of the different freemasonry groups as soon as he made his appearance in Germany. Furthermore, in the eyes of the German public, outside the circle of freemasonry, he appeared from the very beginning as the philosopher par excellence of this dubious sect. Finally, as his books did not carry his name and were signed with a mysterious pseudonym, "The Unknown Philosopher," this enigmatic anonymity favored the rumor that the author or authors of these works were directors of French freemasonry.

Willermoz's activity on behalf of Saint-Martin had a consequence worse yet for the work of the "Unknown Philosopher" in Germany. Willermoz presented himself at the convocation of Wilhelmsbad as representing the most strict observance and the most conservative tendency of the order. By propagating the ideas of his friend Saint-Martin among the adherents of his party, who retained a profound sympathy for theosophy, spiritualism, and occultism, he aroused the suspicion of the opposition, that is of the rationalistic group of the Illumined, against the "Unknown Philosopher." [203]

This group, being inspired by the ideas of Adam Weishaupt, developed a system which was called "natural philosophy," and was animated, not by reason, which they so often claimed, but by an anti-Jesuit mania, according to which the Jesuits, gifted with a superhuman omnipresence, played the role of the Devil. In their eyes, the Unknown Philosopher fell under the same sentence; they discovered that the first letter of the word philosopher was a P; the first letter of the word Inconnu (Unknown) was an I, the whole could be nothing but a monogram, an abbreviation of Peres Jésuites (Jesuit Fathers). [204] Thus, the philosopher Bode, an influential rationalist, who had been at first a member of the Order of Strict Observance, but was later won over by Freiherr Adolf von Knigge to the Order of the Illumined, denounced the members of the theosophical and pietistic school of freemasonry as agents of Jesuit obscurantism and declared that the writings of the Unknown Philosopher were also the products of a crypto-Jesuit intrigue. [205] In 1782, Bode published an anonymous writing under the title **Examen impartial du livre intitulé "Des erreurs et de la vérité" par une frère laïque en fait des sciences.** [206] In it he revealed the Unknown Philosopher's book as a typically Jesuit machination: as proof, he developed a whole secret system of codes which permitted initiates to decipher the true sense and shocking intentions of the Jesuit authors, hidden in deceitful guises. [207]

Thus in Germany, the soil was prepared for a true interest in Saint-Martin's work as well as for a literary scandal, which did not fail to erupt immediately after the appearance of the first translation of his works by Matthias Claudius, the well-known editor of **Wandsbecker Bote,** (The Messenger of Wandsbeck). [208]

Matthias Claudius aroused as many shouts of sympathy as shouts of protest with his first translation of Saint-Martin, published in 1792, under the title, **Irrthümer und Wahrheit, oder Rückweis für die Menschen auf das allgemeine Principium aller Erkenntnis. Von einem unbek. Ph. Aus dem Französischen übersetzt von Matthias Claudius. Mit Churfürstl. Sachsischem gnädigsten Privilegio. Verlegt bey Gottlieb Löwe in Breslau. 1782.**

Probably it was Baron Charles A. G. Kurt von Haugwitz who urged his friend Claudius to make a German translation of the book **Des erreurs et de la vérité,** and who helped him in this work. [209] Haugwitz himself had been for some time a freemason of the Strict Observance, a Rosicrucian, and a practicing alchemist. A friend of the Stolberg brothers, of Lavater, and of Claudius, he was converted, after 1776, to the Moravian community and became, in 1779, with the Grand Duke Charles de Hesse, a member of the "Knights Charitable," that is to say, of the order founded by Willermoz, Saint-Martin's propagandist.

We must remember that the intellectual circles of the Protestant Revival were in contact, sometimes personal contact, with the theosophical and spiritualistic groups of German free-masonry, especially after the decisive split between the Strict Observance groups and the Illumined.

The extraordinary success of Matthias Claudius' literary work is explained by the mediatory position that he kept between the different literary and religious movements of his time. This position was not the result of an intentional conformity, but of a convergence of diverse religious and philosophical positions in his own mind, a convergence which was aided by a certain instinct for ordinary sentiments, commonplace ideas, which permitted him to reduce the boldest inspirations and ideas to a degree suitable to the readers of his **Wandsbecker Bote,** by no means liberated from a certain measure of rationalism in spite of their rejection of rationalist philosophy.

On the one hand, Matthias Claudius maintained the best Lutheran tradition of the Church in Hamburg, not in the sense of formal orthodoxy, but in the sense of pietistic Lutheranism, represented in exemplary manner by Johann Arndt's **Vier Bücher**

vom wahren Christentum, (four books of True Christianity)--books which were, moreover, translated by Zinzendorf himself into French with a dedication to the Cardinal de Noailles. Because of these pietistic elements within his Lutheranism, he was very sensitive to the tendencies of the Evangelical Awakening, which spread from the last decade of the 18th century through all the territorial churches of Germany. He shared with this neopietistic movement a particular aversion to rationalism, to the materialism of modern philosophy and to the rationalist criticism of the Christian religion. On the other hand, he was not blind to the political events of his time. He informed his readers to pay attention to the "signs of the times"--a term from the Apocalypse According to Saint John. He taught them to interpret these signs in a restrained Christian sense, but he taught them to observe them nevertheless. Above all, Matthias Claudius was a personal contact--on a friendly basis--with the great minds of literature, of philosophy, and of the German theology of his time, from Goethe to Wieland, from Klopstock to Hamann, from Jacobi to Kant. Also, his publications had a wide circulation in the most diverse circles.

Claudius concedes in his introduction that the book **Des erreurs et de la vérité** is "strange and difficult to understand" for two reasons: first, the explanation of the origin of evil and man's liberty given in this book seems to him preferable to all other explanations of these problems; next, according to him, the importance of the author does not consist in the word, but rather in the sign:

> Like a mind with closed mouth and forefinger raised, he points out what we do not know; and his signs and warnings are as great and splendid as the summits of well-loved mountains; on the other hand, they are so strange and miraculous that no part of the scope of our reason can be applied to them.

But, Claudius continues, that means nothing:

> It is true that our reason could only lead us into the desert of material nature; but at the point where reason sees itself obliged to give up, the promised land begins to open out. However, it is necessary to guard against taking for lightning what is only a will-o'-the-wisp.

Claudius admits with a certain irony:

> I do not understand this book either; but beyond the impression of stability and serenity, I find a pure will, a sweetness and extraordinary exaltation of sentiment, an inner tranquility and wellbeing; and all that goes right to the heart. He reveals the meaning of the spirit to

> us. He leads us from the visible to the invisible, from
> the ephemeral to the imperishable.

Here Claudius makes allusion to the principal theme of the revival movement formulated by Jung-Stilling:

> Happy are those who suffer nostalgia for the heavenly
> fatherland, since they will return home.

Heimweh (home-sickness) is the nostalgic desire for the heavenly fatherland. Later, Claudius interpreted Saint Martin's **L'Homme du Désir**, in the same sense as desire understood as an ardent longing to return to the heavenly fatherland. He finished the preface of his introduction with the following words:

> Man has a mind which is not satisfied by this world,
> not satisfied to ruminate upon dregs of matter, the thorns
> and thistles along the way, and which wears itself out
> in desire for its fatherland. There is no rest for man,
> and he must die soon. Thus he knows that he would
> be badly served by a wisdom which rests only in visual
> and material nature. He will be satisfied only by what
> is within himself, in his innermost being, immortal as
> he is himself, and which will accompany him like a friend,
> when he dies, through death and decay to his native
> land.

With this introduction, Claudius recommended Saint-Martin's book to the adherents of the Protestant Revival of his time and added it to the great series of edifying books read in the pietistic circles of that time, which were well pleased to discover a French ally in their defense of Christianity against the rationalism and materialism of modern philosophy, which seemed to them to be identical with that of France. Certainly, this interpretation changed the author's own original intention.

The general attitude of the Protestant Revival was to be resigned to the desperate situation of this world, considered as the domain of sin, the Devil and Antichrist and to be consoled with promises of a better beyond, in which the believers would find compensation for all their sufferings in this "vale of tears." [210] This is a completely different emphasis from what one finds in the books of Saint-Martin. He does not underestimate the forces of evil and sin in human history and the depravity of human nature brought about by sin; but his intention is rather to call man back to his original task, the task of becoming the minister of the creative word, of returning to his proper vocation to cooperate with God in his work of perfecting creation in all the spheres of the universe. Saint-Martin's enthusiasm and even optimism did not succeed in inspiring the Revival circles; their emphasis was more on the sentimental elements of the desire, of the nostalgic impetus towards the spiritual world, towards heaven--all this terminology being understood in the bourgeois sense of that time.

The reaction to Saint-Martin's book was spontaneous from all sides. Lavater had already read the original text of the book, in 1779. He did not dare identify himself with its propositions "in part mysterious, in part revolutionary," but he valued the book as an "excellent antidote against materialism" and discovered in it "a second theodicy." He recommended it very highly to Herder. [211]

Herder, once his curiosity was aroused, sought to obtain a copy of the book for himself. But after having read Claudius' translation, he expressed completely negative sentiments to him, and revealed the same unfavorable judgment, in a letter to his friend Knebel, in 1791:

> The book **Des erreurs** has always been abhorrent to me; and I had a disagreement once with Claudius, because of that poison. [212]

In Hamann, to whom Herder had sent his copy, there are signs of the same rejection:

> The transition from transcendental ideas to demonology does not seem very great. Many of the brothers found it more to their taste than I; and now I am told that the lodges are eager to agree. Some prejudices are evident; the arrogant pretence arouses my suspicion even against the good passages that are to be found in it. My mystical concepts of language are very different from those of the author. [213]

The German translation of Saint-Martin was also the occasion for a total disagreement between Claudius and Goethe, whose negative reaction is expressed in the caustic epigram:

> Erreurs et Vérité
>
> Irrtum wolltest du bringen und Wahrheit, O Bote von
>   Wandsbeck.
> Wahrheit, sie war dir zu schwer, Irrtum den brachtest
>   du fort. [214]
>
> You claimed to bring error and truth;
> Truth being too difficult for you, you only brought error.

In 1781, Goethe had already written to Lavater:

> In this book of errors, what truth and what error! The
> most profound mysteries of humanity tied up by the
> straw cords of madness and narrow-mindedness! [215]

So, the older generation was not ready to accept Saint-Martin's philosophy. The rejection by incensed rationalists was even more explicit. Before any favorable reactions appeared, there was a whole series of anonymous pamphlets full of philosophical and political incriminations of all sorts.

The first of these pamphlets is by Johann Joachim Bode, one of Matthias Claudius' first collaborators and co-editors of the **Wandsbecker Bote**, who later split with him and withdrew to a position of strict rationalism. Bode's pamphlet was published in French shortly after the German translation under the title **Examen impartial du livre intitulé Des Erreurs et de la Vérité par un frère laïque en fait de sciences.** A second pamphlet, also anonymous, was published under the title: **Clef des erreurs et de la vérité par un serrurier connu.**, Hersalaim 1789. [217] Charles de Suze is the author of this pamphlet, who also published a **Suite des Erreurs . . . Salomonopolis 1784** (sic). **Le clef des erreurs et de la vérité** was soon published in German, under the title: **Schlüssel des Buchs: Irrthümer und Wahrheit oder Rückweis der Menschen zu dem allgemeinen Princip der Vernunft, von einem bekannten Schlosser,** mit Churfürstl. Sächsischen allergnadigsten Privilegio, Hamburg und Leipzig bey H. J. Matthiessen, 1790.

The well-known Berlin journals soon began a ferocious polemic against Saint-Martin and his unfortunate translator, Matthias Claudius. After Bode, J. E. Biester, famous editor of the **Berlinische Monatsschrift**, published a series of articles against Saint-Martin and Claudius in the years 1785-1789, the very same years, moreover, when some of Kant's well-known essays were published. Saint-Martin and Claudius were similarly exposed to the most vehement attack, in the **Allgemeine Deutsche Bibliothek** published by Friedrich Nicolai, leader of popular rationalism in Germany. Vol. 53 is a journal comprising studies and critical reviews. [218]

Nicolai himself became a victim of the Jesuitophobic myth of the Illumined. On page 160 of the **Berlinische Monatsschrift,** August 1785, he wrote of Saint-Martin:

> There are crafty demagogues who can make diabolical
> use of the mania for dissimulation to gain power for
> themselves. All these men are now zealously preoccupied
> with the book **Des erreurs et de la vérité,** astutely thrown
> out as bait by the French Jesuits, who now flatter them-
> selves by calling themselves Philalèthes. [219]

These denunciations were prevalent throughout Germany.

We will find them in Protestant as well as in Catholic circles. As a single example, I will cite the letter to a friend of Michael Sailer, the head of reformist Catholicism in Bavaria, from the poet Xaver Bronner, which was written in Augsburg on August 24, 1786. In it Bronner gives a detailed description of his encounter with Sailer in Augsburg on the occasion of a balloon ascent. Sailer spoke to him about the book **Des Erreurs et de la vérité**, and Bronner finishes his letter with the following words:

> He must have known that deep in my heart I had an uncontrollable aversion to all types of mysticism and an obvious contempt for all secret sciences; however, he would not let me rest until I was made angry and had given him the sharp reply that I would not allow myself to be hoodwinked by anonymous leaders, perhaps even hidden Jesuits. [220]

The myth took on the character of an epidemic.

These vehement attacks were the cause of an enormous literary polemic, especially on the part of a Protestant theologian who considered it his personal mission to refute this mania among the spokesmen of pure reason. This was the preacher of the court of the Grand Duke of Hessen-Darmstadt, Johann August Starck, who, in the year 1787, published several volumes on crypto-Catholicism, proselytism, Jesuitism, and secret societies. [221] This upright yet aggressive preacher was not content to publish polemical writings against the editors of the **Berlinische Monatsschrift** and the **Allgemeine Deutsche Bibliothek,** but also made accusations against the leaders of rationalism in Berlin and published, in several volumes, the manifold documents of these acrimonious proceedings. [222]

In his books he became the spontaneous advocate not only of Matthias Claudius and Lavater, but also of Saint-Martin, who thus plays a part in a damaging literary scandal concerned with the legal proceedings between the adherents of the Enlightenment and the staunch Protestants defending themselves against succumbing to crypto-Catholicism.

Starck, on whom there is an excellent French thesis by Jean Blum, under the title <u>Johann August Stark et la querelle du crypto-catholicisme en Allemange 1785-1789</u> (Paris, 1914), endeavored to destroy the current myth that after its suppression the Jesuit order would have organized a general campaign to bring down German Protestantism by the infiltration of Catholic ideas and practices into Protestant churches, especially with the aid of secret societies. Starck said:

> It is very difficult to cut a path through these thorny brambles. Everyone adds his own rocks to the piles of rubble: ex-Jesuits, secret societies, Rosicrucians, Illumined, reunion of the churches, Masius, Protestant ministers accused of being secretly Catholics, freemasonry, false toleration, Divine Order, Claudius, magnetism, Cagliostro, Order of the Divine Providence, Lavater, the book **Des erreurs et de la vérité**, Starck, Society for the Propaganda of Pure Doctrine and True Devotion, Templars, secret superiors, Doctor Urlsperger, clerics of the Order of the Temple, Saint Nicaise, Dreycorn, Magic, Knights Beneficent, Obereit, mysticism, alchemists, everything is there pell-mell. **[223]**

Starck does not align himself with Saint-Martin's doctrines nor with Boehme's, which he frankly admits he does not understand; but he takes pleasure in pointing out the absurdity of the accusations hurled against Saint-Martin by the Berlin rationalists. He pretends to accept the key discovered by Bode, which would permit him to disclose the dire crypto-Jesuit machinations of Saint-Martin, and makes use of this key to decipher several lines of Saint-Martin.

> According to the cipher, 'being' no longer signifies being but 'the general of the Jesuits'; 'superior principles' means 'the Jesuit order'; 'man' signifies 'secret societies'; 'beasts,' 'the adversaries of the Jesuits'; 'principle, universal principle, nature, supreme will,' all signify 'the general of the Jesuits'; 'order,' 'name,' 'the mystery of order,' 'God,' always mean 'the general of the Jesuits'; 'the universe,' is 'the sum total of all secret societies.'

So let us translate with the use of this decoder, page 15 of the **Tableau naturel:**

> This first principle also has a freedom which differs essentially from that of other beings; being itself its own law, it can never deviate from it. Thus it does not have this fatal faculty by which man can act against the goal of his existence, which demonstrates the infinite superiority of this universal principle and creator of all law.

According to Bode's key, these lines are deciphered as saying:

> This general of the Jesuits also has a freedom which differs essentially from that of other Jesuit generals, for being himself his own law, he can never deviate from it. Thus, he has not this fatal faculty by which secret societies can act against the goal of their existence, which demonstrates the infinite superiority of the general of the Jesuits, creator of all law.

Where is the Oedipus who could resolve this enigma? [224]

By using the same decoder, Starck performs this same experiment, with some verses from the Apostle Paul with a similar result. After Saint Paul, he takes up the maxims of the Eleatic philosophers with the same result. For example, there is the Eleatic maxim: Nulla res generatur vel corrumpitur, sed speciem tantum eius rei nobis imponit. Evidently, the philosophers meant that the Jesuit order, although outwardly suspended, was immortal and would always continue its activity, despite all defenses against it. He concludes:

> If this truly cabbalistic art of deciphering, exposed by the author in order to decipher the secret intention of the French books (by Saint-Martin) and to reveal the underlying Jesuitism, has any value of its own, evidently there will be no single mystical book by Jacob Boehme, Tauler, Pordage, Johann Arndt, and others of this same type, nor a single philosophical book, nor the Bible, nor the **Berlinische Monatsschrift** itself which is not sure to be understood as allegorical and mystical propaganda from the Jesuit order. [225]

The real influence of Saint-Martin was completely contrary to the denunciations of the rationalists in Berlin. His book was received with the greatest enthusiasm, especially by the adherents of the Protestant Revival and of romantic philosophy. There were even conversions because of Saint-Martin, but in a completely different sense to that suggested by the Illumined: for example, that of Moyse, the son of a Jewish merchant in Hamburg. He was an extremely gifted young man who was converted to the Lutheran church in the wake of reading the translation of Saint-Martin formulated by Matthias Claudius. Moyse gave himself the new Christian name of Neander, that is to say, new man, a name which also represents the central concept of Saint-Martin's book. It is this Neander who later was the famous professor of Protestant theology and who published the book on Saint-Bernard and the mysticism of his time. [226] He was the initiator of a new era in the study of ecclesiastical history, by putting the religious person in the center of Christianity according to the general principle of German romanticism, formulated by Saint-Martin: "It is necessary to explain things by man and not man by things." [227] Soon after Claudius' translation, there were new translations of Saint-Martin's works; and it is especially in the introductions to these German translations that we find the most interesting ideas about Saint-Martin's importance for philosophy and religious life in Germany.

A typical expression of the spirit of the Protestant Revival is to be found in Adolph Wagner, the translator of Saint-Martin's book **L'homme de désir**, published in Leipzig in 1813, under the title **Des Menschen Sehnen und Ahnen.** This book appeared in the midst of the French occupation, during the Napoleonic wars in Prussia and Russia.

First Wagner attacks Saint-Martin's German rationalist enemies, who condemned him as overly enthusiastic and fanatical. He says:

> If one would associate Saint-Martin with the fanatics, whose works are said to come out of an insane asylum, the fault is in the general malady of the era which is called philosophy of enlightenment.

Next, Wagner continues in the tone typical of a revivalist preacher:

> Indeed, it is an extraordinary phenomenon, in an era of frivolous distraction or dull-witted insensibility, in an era of dessicated hearts, amid a nation turned entirely toward the external world, in a language which no longer expresses any 'word of life' (and which speaks more than it says), to encounter a man who, with pious belief, inner composure, gentle sensibility, and delicate sensitivity throughout utters from within his innermost being solemn words on life and love and does so in truly priestly, fervent, edifying terms; lapsing into silence or making gentle allusions rather than raising his voice, he leads us further and further into the depths of the spirit. He is a true pastor in the sense of which there are only a few among us. By returning unceasingly to the one in whom 'we live, move, and have our being' (Acts 17:28), with complete self-denial, with supreme self-sacrifice, with the freest and most zealous renunciation of all that is corporal and temporal, human life appears to him as a process of purification and spiritualization. Borne by powerful flight into the pure sphere of the spirit, lost in an inner intuition, even symbolism is for him only a means and only a spring-board at the lowest level to raise him up from one peak to another to the summit where there are abundant joys and pleasures for evermore. (Ps 16:11).

Wagner finishes by requesting the reader, "not to sweep up the sweet pollen of the flowers of this book with the hard broom of Enlightenment philosophy."

In these phrases formulated in the so-called language of Caanan are to be found all the prejudices of this movement of revival launched against philosophy at a country in which only Saint-Martin was accepted as the great exception.

Another indication of Saint-Martin's adoption by the
Protestant Revival in Germany is the German translation of the
posthumous works of Saint-Martin by D. W. A. Schickedanz, army
chaplain general of Munster in 1833. Of this translation, only
the first part remains, "Die Theosophischen Gedanken," dedicated
to Dr. Siebenbergen of Munster and Dr. Tholuck, famous professor
of theology in the Protestant faculty of the University of Halle,
which still maintained the pietistic tradition of its founder, August
Hermann Francke.

Schickedanz not only translated the two volumes of Saint-
Martin's posthumous works but arranged them systematically in
the way of Pascal's **Pensées**, convinced that Saint-Martin's ideas
were for the German public superior in value even to those of
Pascal:

> Apart from Pascal there is no other French thinker who
> could be compared to Saint-Martin, provided that the
> power of profound thought, full of sublime knowledge
> and Christian sentiments, is taken as the standard of
> comparison. However, in my opinion, Saint-Martin is,
> without doubt, superior to Pascal. It is true that the
> latter was a mathematician of the first order; but his
> thoughts are the only result we have left from his religious
> speculations and they cannot be counterbalanced with
> Saint-Martin's writings, whose content is of no less weight.
> These two minds were inspired as well as sanctified
> by God himself; but Saint-Martin was of a more liberated
> spirit and more removed from the grievous troubles which
> probably contributed to shorten or at least to weaken
> the fine thread of Pascal's life. On the other hand, Saint-
> Martin was very like Pascal, in his truly Christian humility.
> He displayed a rare modesty toward everyone he encoun-
> tered, and everyone was astonished that a man of his
> importance was without any outward show. He was pleasant
> without being superficial and had deep feelings and emo-
> tions of human kindness. According to the editors of
> his posthumous works, he was a true Christian by doctrine
> as well as by life, a friend of God and man. [228]

Proceeding from this general idea of Saint-Martin's importance, Schickedanz arranged the parts of his posthumous works,
under the following headings: "God," "Grace," "Faith," "Original
Sin," "Penitence," "Conversion and Regeneration," "Prayer," "Love,"
"Marriage and the Sexes," "Sufferings and Afflictions," "Death
and Eternal Life," "Science," "Philosophy and Literature," "Psychol-
ogy," "Politics," and "Autobiographical Notes."

By this arrangement, Schickedanz transformed Saint-
Martin's posthumous works into a book of spiritual instruction

or catechism according to the style of the Evangelical Revival. He wrote:

> In regard to the following work, I am convinced that Saint-Martin's thoughts are worth reading, first because of the author himself, one of the first theosophers of all time and the most profound thinker of modern France . . . But the principal reason for their value is to be found in their content which is so excellent that they could serve as a book of spiritual instruction for Christian thinkers. They should not be upset by the fact that Saint-Martin's ideas are sometimes close to the paradoxical; in this way the author's style is in agreement with Hamann. Let the true spiritual life which is in communion with its source be augmented by the reading of these writings!

Schickedanz's general idea of Saint-Martin's position in contemporary French philosophy corresponds to the above estimation of his works. He considers Saint-Martin as the great exception to the general philosophical tendencies of his time:

> This man, of whose posthumous works we have given a selection, is one of the most remarkable and superior. At the very moment in France when the false wisdom of Voltaire and the Encyclopedists was attempting to exterminate religious life and especially all Christian life and when they had been successful among most of their compatriots, Saint-Martin was one of the most important and most successful apologists in the challenge to Christianity . . . He was not by profession a scholar of the church and followed a completely different line of work. [229]

> It was not simple opposition to the irreligious philosophy of his time which provoked his activity--one extreme provoking the other--for Saint-Martin came from a theosophical school already in existence, firm and encouraging evidence that the Lord has his people, who never died out, even in France. The existence of this theosophical school developed by Saint-Martin is a remarkable thing in itself. The French and theosophers, what a contradiction at first sight! But it is certain that the French also have a talent for speculation and a depth of intellect--after all Pascal did write his thoughts--although these qualities are not very widespread in France. [230]

In Saint-Martin's biography, there were two points which particularly attracted his translator's interest: the first is Saint-Martin's attitude to the French Revolution, and the other is his French translation of Jacob Boehme.

Because of the generally hostile interpretation of the French Revolution in the circles of philosophy, he gave an explanation as theatrical as it is questionable of Saint-Martin's interest in it. He says:

> Saint-Martin lived mostly in Paris during the Revolution, in part because most of his friends remained there and in part because he wished to fight against the false philosophy of the time at its source as Saint Paul and Saint Peter proclaimed the Gospel at the source of paganism in Rome. [231]

Another time he describes the philosopher Saint-Martin in Paris during the troubles of the Revolution "as a Christian Archimedes during the assault of Syracuse." [232] It was typical of the spiritual situation of the time to strive to put as much distance as possible between the "Unknown Philosopher," who represented the great exception in French philosophy, and the French Revolution, enfant terrible of French materialist and rationalist philosophy.

As for Jacob Boehme, Schickedanz gives first a detailed description of Saint-Martin's encounter with his work. He writes that Saint-Martin became acquainted with Boehme's writings during his stay in Strasburg, thanks to a kind Christian lady, when he was close to fifty years of age; that he learned German particularly in order to understand him better; and that he reached such perfection in German that he was able to translate the major part of Boehme's works:

> Anyone who has read Jacob Boehme and knows the difficulty of understanding his writings, by virtue of the profundity of their content, and also by reason of the awkwardness and obscurity of their style, a fact which is not surprising, since the brilliant author had no higher education; added to which a good part of this language was already completely out-dated, while many of the technical terms were invented by the author himself (so that there is no dictionary we can use). When considering all these obstacles, anyone who knows this will be astonished that Saint-Martin familiarized himself with this language so quickly and so completely. His translations are perfect, and one can say without exaggeration that even for the German reader who wishes to study Jacob Boehme, it is helpful to use along side the original text the French translation whose language is of the same clarity and beauty as the rest of Saint-Martin's writings. [233]

And Schickedanz finished with Saint-Martin's testimony that his first teacher, Pasqually, showed him half of the truth and from afar, whereas Jacob Boehme revealed it to him completely and up close. [234]

The third group upon which Saint-Martin had a strong and direct influence is the Catholic reform group, which had its spiritual leader in Bishop Sailer of Regensburg. [235] German Catholicism was open to influences similar to those which we find in full activity in the Evangelical Revival among Protestant churches, Lutheran as well as Reformed. In the Catholic circles of Southern Germany, Bavaria, and Swabia, there were the same mystical tendencies as in the Protestant circles: the return to the definite value of a personal appropriation of the Gospel; the recommendation to read the Bible and especially the New Testament in German; the insistence on personal religious experience; the recognition of visions and individual personal inspiration; the discovery and encouragement of parapsychic phenomena of religion; the idea of personal renewal as the unique basis of true Christian life; the gathering together into circles of "true Christians" where, in Catholic circles as well as in the Protestant gatherings, the "reborn" recount their spiritual experiences and encourage the communication and sharing of devout feelings and mystical ideas. In the Catholic circles, there was no claim to be antihierarchical, although there was a general inclination to emphasize the spiritual values of the church understood as the mystical body and to devaluate the proper meaning of the Church's canonical institutions or concede to them a more symbolic sense.

The leaders of this Catholic Revival were personally linked with the leaders of the similar movement in the Protestant churches. Sailer was in correspondence with Jung-Stilling at Marburg as well as with Lavater in Zürich and Matthias Claudius in Hamburg. [236] Sailer could not avoid a heresy trial during his activity as professor of theology at the Catholic Institute of Dillingen, especially when several Catholic priests such as Martin Boos, Johann Gossner, Ignaz Lindl, pupils of Sailer, introduced forms increasingly Protestant into their worship in several parishes in the diocese of Augsburg and ended by making a total break with their ecclesiastical superiors and emigrating with most of their adherents to Russia, where the Czar Alexander I himself, caught up in the Evangelical Revival, under the influence of Madame de Krüdener and Jung-Stilling, had granted them free exercise of their worship and free land for colonization. We should remember that Johannes Baptista Gossner, the founder of the Gossnerian Protestant Mission of Berlin, which is still fully active today in India and Africa, was one of these Catholic priests who, as students of Sailer, emigrated to Russia after the controversy with their Catholic superiors in Augsburg. Gossner was the preacher at the Catholic Church of Saint Petersburg, where he was the originator of an evangelical revival among the Orthodox, Catholics, and Protestants of the city, and founded a great ecumenical community, which lasted until his expulsion from Saint Petersburg. [237]

It is understandable that someone like Saint-Martin should be well received in the circles of reform Catholicism, and that he should be considered as an ally. It was especially because of his spiritualistic and mystical tendencies that he was appreciated by the German Catholics of this group. Here was a French Catholic who had himself participated in the Revolution, who did not represent the formalistic and reactionary Catholicism of the French emigrants, and who proclaimed a spiritual and even progressive interpretation of the Gospel at the very moment when the administration of the French Church had been disorganized by the events of the Revolution and when the philosophy of the Revolution had created its own cult of reason!

Sailer seems to have become acquainted with Saint-Martin's works thanks to his friend, Konrad Schmid, professor of law at Dillingen. We have a letter from Franz Xaver Bronner, author of idyllic poetry, dated August 24, 1786, which shows us Sailer as a propagandist of different theosophical books. There is also a denunciatory letter from the pen of one of Sailer's colleagues. In this letter, dated February 21, 1787, he writes:

> Sailer had requested several small works concerning magic, astrology, mysticism, and even freemasonry from his friends, my overseer, von den Heiden, and Ruesch, the secret counselor, to Oettingen and others. I do not know what use he made of them, but during my sojourn at Dillingen he recommended the book **Des erreurs et de la vérité** in particular, to a student named Amand Widenmann, who presented it to me on February 21, 1787, adding: 'Sailer highly recommended this book to me, and told me he found much wisdom there each time he read it.' [238]

The denunciatory character of this letter is obvious: to recommend a book such as Saint-Martin's to a student of the Catholic Institute, who should rather be protected from such reading, seemed a crime to Sailer's colleague.

Sailer's books show us very clearly the influence that Saint-Martin's philosophy had over him. But at this time what interests us more are Sailer's letters after he became bishop, when, after submitting to a very vigorous examination of his orthodoxy at the end of his career as professor of theology at Dillingen and after having been reaffirmed, he still continued to interest his friends in Saint-Martin's philosophy and to discuss it with them with complete freedom. The most interesting correspondents from this point of view are Clemens Brentano and Friedrich Karl von Savigny, the one a great romantic poet, the other the great philosopher of jurisprudence and also representative of romanticism in the jurisprudence of the time, a colleague of Sailer for several years at Landshut before his nomination to Berlin in 1810.

On March 16, 1815, Sailer wrote to his Protestant friend, Clemens Brentano:

> Your theosophical reflections in the manner of Jacob Boehme and Saint-Martin are very fine, Christian, and interpreted according to the concept of apostolic Christianity. [239]

This proves to us that even after his heresy trial, Sailer was always ready to accept the concepts of Boehme and Saint-Martin as elements of an apostolic, that is to say, spiritual Christianity, even if not identified with the canonical forms of the Roman Church.

The correspondence between Sailer and his friend Friedrich Karl von Savigny, also a Protestant, shows us that the professor of Landshut was not only concerned with recommending Saint-Martin's books to his friends, and with enabling them to purchase these books, but also with lending them his own copies which he had purchased dearly or received as gifts from other friends. [240] Truly, he was at the center of the circulation of Saint-Martin's books within the important intellectual circles in Germany at that time: among romantic poets, among scholars attracted by the romantic movement, and among the adherents of the Catholic and Evangelical Revival.

The German translation of the work in which Saint-Martin's Christian spiritualism finds its freest expression was undertaken by a Catholic who himself belonged to a reform group of German Catholicism, and who was finally excommunicated as one of the protagonists of the resistance against Roman ultramontanism and against the dogma of papal primacy, Johann Anton Bernhard Lutterbeck. [241]

b. 1812

Born in 1812, near Munster, he studied Catholic theology at Munster and became professor of Catholic theology at the University of Giessen, where a Catholic theological faculty had recently been inaugurated. This new institution in a purely Protestant setting provided the opportunity to open the small faculty to all sorts of liberal influences. Lutterbeck became the protagonist of Hermesianism, of the concepts of Professor Hermes of Cologne, who wanted to replace traditional scholastic philosophy with modern critical philosophy in the interpretation of Catholic dogma. [242] Lutterbeck was attacked by his ecclesiastical superiors in the bishopric of Mainz, and was obliged to give up his preaching in the Mainz diocese. Suspect because of Lutterbeck's dogmatic aberrations, the Catholic faculty of Giessen was closed down by the bishop of Mainz, Ketteler. Later, Lutterbeck participated very actively in the opposition to the First Vatican Council and in the German Catholic professors' protest against the decrees of this council on papal primacy, and afterwards allied himself with the Old Catholic movement.

However, at the time of his translation, Lutterbeck scrupled at the translation of Saint-Martin's pages in which the criticism of the Catholic Church's formalism and institutionalism was expressed too freely and in terms too bold for his own liking. This applied particularly to the great controversy with Chateaubriand, which appears in this work by Saint-Martin.

One of the most surprising things in this time of spiritual relationships between France and Germany is the fact that Saint-Martin influenced German Catholicism much more than did Chateaubriand. Today we are inclined to think the contrary and believe that the acclaim of the Génie du christianisme was as spontaneous on the part of German Catholics as of those in France. [243] But the facts show us a completely different situation. It is true that there was already a first German translation of this book in 1803-1804 in Munster, a second in Munich in 1820, and a third in Mainz in 1828; but their authors are unknown--Karl Heinrich Georg Venturini is the author of the first translation, at Munster--or anonymous; and it is very significant that neither in Franz von Baader, Sailer, nor Matthias Claudius is there the slightest reference to Chateaubriand, whereas Saint-Martin is on everyone's lips and cited and discussed in the works and letters of these well-known writers.

The principal reason for this phenomenon was that the general situation of Catholicism in Germany was completely different from that of French Catholicism. In France, it was necessary to rediscover and re-establish the beauty of a Catholicism debased and desecrated by the Revolution and to reconstruct its liturgical base in the practice of the religious life--that is what Chateaubriand did. In Germany, the political and social situation of Catholicism changed little: there, the great danger was what Franz von Baader called "petrification," a purely external and conventional institutionalism. What was necessary was not a return to pompous liturgy, but an interiorization, a spiritualization, a new interpretation of dogmas inspired by mystical experience and by the personal intuition of the faithful. That is why there was an inclination to give a cordial welcome to Saint-Martin's works and ideas; he was considered the representative of a kind of Catholicism interiorized and spiritualized as a result of the troubles of the Revolution, which could serve as a model for a transformation of petrified German Catholicism, a tranformation which the reform circles eagerly desired.

Saint-Martin himself was very conscious of the strong tension existing between his own conception of Christianity and that of Chateaubriand. His reaction to Génie du christianisme was very outspoken and, in an impassioned polemic, gradually led him to much more radical conclusions than he had at first envisioned. This controversy with Chateaubriand is found in the work **Le ministère de l'homme-esprit,** which appeared in 1802, the same year as **Génie du christianisme,** and represented the immediate response to this work.

Lutterbeck, who was himself inclined to accept such a criticism, lacked the courage to publish it in his translation of Saint-Martin's work, because at that particular time he hoped to avoid a definite confrontation with his superiors. Thus, he says in his introduction to Saint-Martin, pp. viii-ix:

> In order to judge him correctly, we must consider the spirit rather than the letter. There are many men, whose words are quite orthodox in form, but whose intent is at fault, since their heart is far away from what their lips are saying. Others have the truth in their hearts, but burning with zeal for the house of the Lord, their mouths can do nothing but babble . . . They say what they do not intend to say. That happened to our writer, especially in the pages of this book, where he declares he is against Chateaubriand and his too superficial, too romantic, and too sensually Catholic Christianity in utterly inadequate terms, and where he opens up a polemic against what is petrified in Catholicism, which goes too far, and throws the baby out with the bath water--or throws out the gold with the dross--and totally forgets that the petrified are very often the only conservationists. Because of this inaccuracy and since Saint-Martin retracted his excessive criticism in his posthumous works, we felt obliged to omit these pages from our translation. However, if someone is interested in them, he can read them in the original text. [**244**]

If, following Lutterbeck's suggestion, we consult the original text, we are surprised to verify that Lutterbeck omitted more than twenty pages which are, in truth, the most concise expression of the spiritualist interpretation of Christianity, opposed here to the spirit of restoration expressed by Chateaubriand. The reproaches hurled against Chateaubriand are concentrated in Saint-Martin in the charge of having confused Christianity with Catholicism; and to illustrate this confusion, he gives a whole series of differences between Christianity and Catholicism. This series begins with differences of degree which prove that Catholicism has not yet succeeded in realizing the intention and primordial form of Christianity. But more and more the difference of degree is transformed into a difference of nature, and it ends in a full spiritual rebellion against the "petrified" institution of Catholicism.

In the criticism of Chateaubriand which is found in **Le ministère de l'homme-esprit**, by Saint-Martin, p. 368, the following words were omitted in the German translation:

> The principal reproach that I have to make is that at every step Christianity is confused with Catholicism.

Here is a list of the differences between Christianity and Catholicism:

1. Christianity is merely the very spirit of Jesus Christ in its fullness.

2. Catholicism, to which the title of religion properly belongs, is the way of ordeal and toil to reach Christianity.

3. Christianity is the region of deliverance and liberty: Catholicism is only the seminary of Christianity; it is the place of rules and discipline for the neophyte.

4. Christianity carries our faith into the luminescent region of the eternal divine word; Catholicism restricts this faith to the limits of the written word or traditions.

5. Christianity exalts and extends the use of our rational faculties. Catholicism constrains and circumscribes the exercise of these same faculties.

6. Christianity shows us God is to be discovered in the depths of our being, without the aid of forms and formulae. Catholicism leaves us to contend with ourselves to find God hidden beneath the pomp of ceremony.

7. Christianity has no mysteries; and that very word would be repugnant to it, since by nature Christianity is evidence and universal clarity. Catholicism is full of mysteries and rests only on an indiscernible foundation. The Sphinx can be placed on the threshold of temples, constructed by the hand of man; it cannot sit on the threshold of man's heart, which is the true entrance door for Christianity.

Christianity is the fruit of the tree; Catholicism can only be its fertilizer (= Dung).

Christianity has no sects, since it embraces unity; and this unity being single, it cannot be divided within itself. Catholicism has seen fit to give birth to multitudes of schisms and sects which have advanced more the reign of division than that of concord; and this Catholicism itself, when it believes itself to be at the most perfect degree of purity, finds hardly two of its members who have a common belief.

> Christianity has incited war only against sin; Catholicism has incited it against men.
>
> Christianity makes its way only by genuine and continuing experiences; Catholicism makes its way only by the regulations of authorities and institutions. Christianity is only the law of faith; Catholicism is only faith in the law.
>
> . . . . . .
>
> Christianity belongs to eternity; Catholicism belongs to time.
>
> Christianity is the end; Catholicism, despite the imposing majesty of its solemn observances, and despite the saintly magnificence of its worthy prayers, is only the means. [245]

Evidently, at that particular time, Lutterbeck did not wish to translate these lines. On the other hand, we can understand that it would be precisely pages such as these that would attract the interest and the most lively sympathy from the circles of the Evangelical Protestant Revival and also from theosophical circles, which adhered to a purely spiritual ecclesiology and had been accustomed to launch similar criticism against their own institutions of territorial churches from the time of Gottfried Arnold.

Saint-Martin maintained his spiritual interpretation of Christianity up until the last moment of his life; and, on his death bed, he refused the presence of a priest and extreme unction, since he considered himself beyond the sphere of rites and symbols by reason of his personal initiation into the spiritual mysteries of Christianity.

This same need to find excuses for Saint-Martin's spiritual elements, is found in another Catholic writer of this era, Friedrich Schlegel, the friend of Schleiermacher, who, during his stay in Cologne in 1804, leaned more and more towards Catholicism and publicly converted to the Catholic Church, under the direct influence of the ideas of Saint-Martin. As proof of Saint-Martin's orthodoxy, Lutterbeck took the fact of Friedrich Schlegel's conversion to Catholicism which he expressed in the following words: "Friedrich von Schlegel was led by him to a positive idea of the world." [246]

Friedrich von Schlegel attested to the orthodoxy of Saint-Martin's religious philosophy in his **Geschichte der alten und neuen Literatur**, where the following judgment on Saint-Martin is found:

> Already before and during the Revolution, Saint-Martin, under the name Unknown Philosopher, in a series of works which remained unnoticed by the masses, but which

produced an effect all the more profound upon a minority, re-established the old system of spiritualism, which appears in our time as a novelty. However, the reproach made to him of being, as a Catholic, a moderate opponent of the ecclesiastical constitution is based upon appearance rather than on the facts. And if this reproach can be hurled more deservedly against some of its adherents in France or in Russia, that is not surprising, since the successors and disciples of a great man usually take from their master something quite different from a wise moderation. But if Saint-Martin did not approve of the current state of ecclesiastical affairs, it was with reason during those revolutionary times made more so because of the unhappy years before; and the general situation of those times gave him sufficient excuse. However, the misunderstanding as such is still unacceptable, and contrary to the great aim of religion, which was his principal objective, by producing the erroneous appearance that knowledge of God should be based only on perception and purely inner intuition and that it could be separated, or at least moved further from the positive tradition of the visible church understood as their natural representa- tive and essential form. But nowhere, did Saint-Martin pit true knowledge in opposition to religion in a hostile sense or hold it up in opposition to the latter (religion). He does not cease to express the desire that superior knowledge should become totally the property and instru- ment of religion and be one with the priesthood. This attitude is the sign more of the high value he places on the vocation of the priesthood than of his contempt for the ordinary rules of the dominant spirit of the century and for a common and carnal philosophy, which he never ceased to resist during his whole lifetime. But all that is concerned only with external circumstances; Saint- Martin's doctrine is never in opposition to the system of Catholic faith itself; it is in perfect accord with it, all the more as his philosophy is not only Mosaic, but also truly Christian. If, then, this writer . . . strictly speaking should not have the glory of having invented this Christian philosophy which he took as his own, if some errors infiltrated his interpretation it is still remark- able that in the middle of France at that time filled with atheism, a philosophy appeared which was exclusively concerned with refuting this same atheistic philosophy and that it should put in opposition to it a Mosaic and Christian philosophy divinely revealed and based on an ancient sacred tradition. Let us rejoice to see that among so many spokesmen of the Catholic cause, the first among them, the Count de Maistre, finally had the intelligence to notice what treasure of intellect and understanding, if one made good use of it, was hidden there. [247]

Thus, Schlegel was well aware of the spiritualistic tendencies in his spiritual father; but after his conversion he preferred to give them a completely favorable interpretation, which permitted him to maintain his orthodoxy in the eyes of his orthodox contemporaries who were very discriminating with regard to a convert.

Franz von Baader was the German thinker who both introduced Saint-Martin's principal ideas in the most direct and succinct way into German idealistic philosophy and was the protagonist of the French works as well as of their German translations.

Baader did not become familiar with Saint-Martin's ideas through the works of the Unknown Philosopher, but by an introduction at the hand of his friend, Johann Friedrich Kleuker, the well-known professor of theology at the University of Kiel, a friend of Claudius, Jacobi and Hamann, who introduced the comparative history of religions into Protestant theology. [248] Kleuker was the first to translate into German the French edition of the **Zent Avesta** by Anquetil Duperron, and published the first German book on the religious system of the Brahmins according to the [Hindu] work of Paulinus a S. Bartholomeo (1797). Kleuker, who also had a profound knowledge of the ancient and modern cabalistic traditions, contributed his share to the propagation of Saint-Martin's ideas, by his book **Magikon** (1784). In the first part, Kleuker gives an exposition of Saint-Martin's doctrine as found in his works **Des erreurs** and **Tableau naturel** (1775 and 1782); in the second part, he gives a positive criticism of his theosophical system, with many notes and additions. Baader had the highest opinion of his friend Kleuker's work and commented on it in his private copy by adding many marginal notes, sometimes long explanations which were published by Baron von Osten-Sacken in the twelfth volume of **The Complete Works of Baader.** [249]

Twelve years later in a letter to Kleuker in Munich, November 6, 1804, Baader recalls very clearly this first encounter, when he writes:

> More than twelve years have elapsed since I read for the first time your work **Magikon,** and since that time, I have never been without it in the course of my continual travels. It provided the permanent direction for my intellect; primarily it awakened in me the taste and feeling for learning and the aspiration to knowledge which justly coincides with the aspiration to be good. Indeed, I have not made the acquaintance of another writer who would have treated this subject in a manner so thorough, so instructive, and so comprehensible; and I would have very much liked to speak with him personally on this subject and receive more information from him.

> But due to the fact that I was prevented from visiting him on my last return from England, and that I now find myself under some sort of obligation to study this subject more seriously than ever, I am lacking the instruction and information of an expert. You will not take it badly if in all confidence I address myself to you as your pupil and if I beseech you to give me from the treasure of your own experience and your literary knowledge information on the method and discipline for the studies necessary for this purpose . . . Tired of meandering on the surface, battered by winds and storms and among so many tiresome companions, I yearn to bury myself in the tranquil and peaceful depths, where one finds little company, but where only real treasures are to be obtained. [250]

It is surprising to find that the spontaneous and ever increasing interest that Franz von Baader confesses in the Unknown Philosopher encouraged him to seek out personal contact with Saint-Martin. He gives us some other details about these attempts in the same letter to Kleuker, where he continues:

> Your judgment on Saint-Martin's system was essentially confirmed in his varied works recently published; at the same time these have convinced me that he lacks structure and would have done better to follow Bacon's method. It was only a little before his death that I found his address; I wrote him a long letter, but unfortunately it found him no longer among the living. [251]

Baader also speaks of the efforts he made to have a personal contact with Saint-Martin, in his correspondence with another theosopher friend, Charles de Meyer, with whom he discussed at length the problems of magnetism, somnambulism, and the visions of Swedenborg. On March 2, 1816, he writes from Schavabing:

> And here, Sir, is another query concerning knowledge: I presume that you could tell me something about Martinez de Pasqually, something more precise than I have been able to learn up to this point. For I had only one single encounter with Saint-Martin himself and that by letter, although I had the intention of visiting him in Paris a short time before his death. I beseech you, then, as much as is possible by letters, to give me some information on the system of numbers that Saint-Martin learned from his teacher Pasqually--yet Saint-Martin soon veered in another direction and ended up not by becoming the Pascal, but the Rousseau of mysticism. Whatever it is, then, that you could and would be willing to share with

me on the doctrines of Pasqually and Saint-Martin, I will use with gratitude. [252]

The fact that it was always a matter of private and secret information from one brother freemason-theosopher to another is shown in the form of the salutation at the end of this letter to his friend and colleague:

One with you in the spirit of brotherhood in the silent but everlasting work of the construction of the Lord's temple, I sign with true devotion, etc.

Baader's second encounter with Saint-Martin's work took place very soon, at the time of the great scandal provoked by the German translation of the book **Des erreurs et de la vérité**. There is a first mention in Baader's private journal dated January 31, 1787. This shows us that Baader, after having personally read the above-mentioned work, did not accept the criticism hurled against the Unknown Philosopher in the journal edited by Pfenninger, [253] friend and colleague of Lavater, the champion of Swiss Protestant orthodoxy. Pfenninger published **Sammlungen zu einem christlichen Magazin** with reviews of theological books recently published. In Volume II, Part 2, 1782 (p. 193) he published a review of the book **Des erreurs** and later in Vol. IV, Part 2, 1784 (pp. 187-223) a review of **Tableau naturel** with some very scathing criticism from the orthodox point of view. He considered the book **Des erreurs** to be the foreboding of a dreadful superstition; the work aroused in him "the sad presentiments of a vandalism threatening all of Europe"; he found in it warning signs announcing that biblical prophecies would soon be fulfilled and that the deadly forces of unbelief and superstition would ultimately produce anti-Christianity which would be determined to annihilate Christianity and to prepare the unqualified triumph of the Anti-Christ. [254]

Baader refuses to accept this criticism and says:

Without doubt, these men--such as Pfenninger and his collaborators--must know of other less questionable and more convincing facts than those on which they based this anathema. In regard to the book itself, I find myself in agreement with Claudius, and with the author of **Magi-kon**, on the fact that it is impossible to find this Satanic doctrine in it; on the contrary, repeated reading of this book makes me return each time with a greater joy to the Bible, just as from each well-written book on nature I come back to nature itself with a fresh joy and new desire. In **Des erreurs et de la vérité**, many readers have already found many things. As for me, I regard the sum of its content as a very reasonable commentary on the words of our Lord: 'Without me, you can do nothing.' (Jn 15:5)

It is true that there is a pseudognosis; and the work **Tableau naturel,** a book which can by no means be called anti-messianic, speaks to us clearly enough of one such school of Satan spreading out dreadfully among us; but that is exactly why there is and why there was always a true gnosis. Did not our Savior himself reveal to us these laws of infinite nature, these paternal laws, for example in speaking of himself, his mission, and his future?--all mysteries of nature--'In truth I tell you this, if the grain of corn which is fallen onto the ground does not die, it remains alone; but if it dies, it bears much fruit.' (Jn 12:24). In these words he reveals to his disciples the Father in heaven and the analogy of his sublime advance in the moral and physical world. And I am not at all convinced that it would be wrong or dishonest in our time or that it would be the sign of a vain philosophy to describe more clearly the sublime advance of the analogy, the principal key of the universe, to unbelievers, to Turks and to Christians, and to melt the icy barriers before their eyes. [255]

Baader finds himself confirmed in his judgment of Saint-Martin by the fact that the very same author was attacked from the side of the rationalists, the Illumined, "the most insolent Socinians of our century." In the face of all Saint-Martin's adversaries, whom he seems to have studied with great care, Baader finishes with the following words:

But it remains certain that in these two books, Saint-Martin declared truths which must be received as Gospel welcome to every Christian; (they are) obviously brilliant truths, but why would they have to be less evangelical because they are brilliant? Are not the truths issuing from Christ's mouth all as brilliant as the sun in the sky? Truly, it would be too much if under this garment of light were hid a heinous Abaddon (Rev 9:11); and as a Christian and a lover of divine wisdom I invite each of my colleagues to show me places which would force me, against my will, to seek the spirit of these books outside instead of within them! Until now, I have considered it my task not to condemn these works and not to denounce their unknown author as being inspired by Satan because of the brilliant truths which are undeniably there. Each testimony for the Lord to whom 'all power has been given in heaven and in earth' (Matt 28:18) is true and holy if it excites in us a true desire for him, a desire not for the testimony, but for the one who is testified. In me, the writer of these works truly aroused this desire.

Several weeks afterward, he did not hesitate to compare

the Unknown Philosopher to the magi and wisemen of the East, with an obvious allusion to the freemason-theosophical character of the writings; and he wrote:

> Who knows if the magi from the East did not find the infant sooner than you others, scribes and scholars in Israel, who no longer need this key? Are you not in actual fact plunged into a mortal dogmatic slumber similar to that of your colleagues of bygone times? And does it not seem that strangers both in appearance and clothing will be obliged to wake you from it? [256]

The result of Baader's studies on Saint-Martin are found in the twelfth volume of Franz von Baader's complete works, edited by his pupil Franz Hoffmann. This volume was edited by a Baltic theosopher, Baron Friedrich von Osten-Sacken, from Wormen in Kurland. In this volume, the same baron published an excellent introduction dealing with Saint-Martin's influence on Baader's philosophy, an introduction which is the best essay in existence on this subject. [257]

The publication of this twelfth volume caused great difficulties because there were no complete texts on Saint-Martin among Baader's posthumous papers, but much material in the form of notes, commentaries, and especially Baader's marginal notes in his copies of the original text or of different German translations published up to 1840. Thus we have continual commentaries on Saint-Martin's works from the hand of Franz von Baader. On the one hand, these notes and comments give us precise information about the ideas of Saint-Martin which seemed to him the most important and the most significant to be carried over into his own theories; and on the other hand they show us the transformation or the "creative misunderstanding" of some of Saint-Martin's other ideas to Baader's own system.

Besides these notes and commentaries, Baader contributed to the spread of Saint-Martin's ideas by specific writings.

First, he published an edition of Saint-Martin's address on the topic posed by the National Institute of Paris: "Déterminer l'influence des signes sur la formation des idées." ("Define the influence of symbols on the formation of ideas.") (1799). The address contains the proof of two theosophical principles: 1. that symbols stimulate and elicit ideas, but do not create them; 2. that before sin, there existed a primitive language composed of fixed and comprehensive symbols, of which actual languages are only an incomplete copy. Baader published a German edition of this address in Friedrich von Schlegel's review Concordia, Part 2, 1820-21, under the title: "Über den Einfluss der Zeichen der Gedanken auf deren Erzeugung und Gestaltung." [258]

This same Baader gave to his friend Gottfried Heinrich von Schubert, the author of the well-known book about the soul, the idea of developing a German translation of Saint-Martin's work **De l'esprit des choses ou coup d'oeil philosophique sur la nature des êtres et sur l'objet de leur existence,** (Paris, Year VIII, 1800, 2 Vol.). This work itself was inspired by Jacob Boehme's **De Signatura Rerum,** in which Saint-Martin gives a new, more complete, and more profound exposition of the mystical doctrine of universal symbolism or the analogy and the correspondence between the natural and spiritual worlds. Schubert published this two-volume translation through Reclam in Leipzig, 1811-12.

Baader wrote an enthusiastic introduction to his friend Schubert's translation and thus contributed by his own reputation as a philosopher to the propagation of this book. He followed the translation from its beginnings with encouraging letters, such as that of June 30, 1810, when he wrote to Schubert:

> It is with pleasure that I wait for your translation of **L'esprit des choses,** by which you will give great pleasure to many souls eager for enlightenment. [259]

Baader proposed to Schubert that he should also prepare a German translation of Saint-Martin's work, **Le ministere de l'homme-esprit** and offered to contribute notes and commentaries to it. [260]

In Baader's introduction to **L'esprit des choses,** translated by Schubert, we find the same interpretation of Saint-Martin's work that we have already observed in Claudius: in his opinion, Saint-Martin is very clearly distinguishable from the general rationalistic and materialistic tendency of the contemporary philosophy and maintains a quite exceptional avant-garde position as a Christian theosopher. Baader expressed this state of affairs in somewhat exaggerated images, which, however offensive they may appear, give us an idea of the general spirit of this period in romantic philosophy. In his introduction he writes:

> It cannot be denied that especially in France the spawning time of this bogus frog (Enlightenment philosophy) gave its first products with such abundance that all of Europe was swamped by materialistic systems and abnegators of God and nature. We should rejoice all the more to see enter on the scene . . . a writer who revealed the ancient doctrine of harmony between enlightenment from nature and that from grace--according to Bacon's expression--a doctrine which was proclaimed by the so-called mystics and theosophers of all ages, but which was a scandal to the Pharisees and foolishness to the Sadducees (I Cor 1:23)--and all this, in part in a new garment

and in part with a greater success than all predecessors. The immortal worth of this writer, persecuted for his work during his lifetime, appears even greater to us if we consider the obstacles he had to overcome in his own time, in his environment and even in the language that he used to express this type of truth. Is there a more risky and more difficult undertaking than to compose words of life to a funeral hymn?

In the face of these different interpretations, can it be said that Saint-Martin was really unrecognized or badly understood in Germany? I do not believe so. Even the pietistic category, into which he was sometimes put, did not prevent the best minds among his adherents from pushing his ideas to an extreme because of the theosophical heritage of German pietism, which was preserved from the time of Oetinger until the era of neopietism at the beginning of the 19th century. Fortunately, within Saint-Martin's writings, there were warnings to put the reader on guard against a common pietistic interpretation.

If we look at the texts, in which Saint-Martin himself speaks of the intention of his philosophy and of his own situation in the middle of his era, we see that he was particularly conscious of having a mission and a specific vocation, which gave him an exceptional character in his own eyes. He considers himself as the "sweeper of the temple of truth" and as such "I must not be surprised at having so many against me; the sweepings defend themselves against the broom as much as they can." [261]

This consciousness of fulfilling a vocation contrary to the spirit of the times developed sometimes into the idea of a total isolation in the midst of a hostile world, where he waits for the vessel to carry him away from his place of exile:

When I consider the state of man in this world below and my personal situation in the midst of so many mortals from whom I can expect no spiritual aid and for whom I am not able to provide any, it occurred to me to regard myself, where I am, as the Robinson of spirituality and obliged, like him, to provide alone for my subsistence, to defend myself from ravenous animals, and to use my whole being ceaselessly for my preservation and for my maintenance. But I have found for myself, as did he, an assurance which provides me with consolations and a strong hope that one day some kind ship will come to take me from my desert island. [262]

Sometimes this feeling of isolation reaches despair. At the time of the publication of his book **Le ministère de l'homme-esprit** towards the end of 1802, he writes in a state of complete resignation:

> Although this work is clearer than the others, it is still
> too far from humanist ideas for me to count upon its
> success. While writing it, I often felt it was as if I were
> playing waltzes and quadrilles on my violin in the cemetery
> at Montmartre, where I wielded my bow in vain as the
> corpses heard nothing of my notes and did not dance. [263]

This feeling of isolation is shown sometimes in the notion
that his contemporaries rejected him with hostile intent. Perhaps,
this is the source of his affinity with Rousseau, that great unappre-
ciated recluse:

> Someone said to Rousseau, who wished to speak: 'They
> will not hear you.' One could say the same thing to
> me and add: 'They do not wish to hear you,' without
> taking into account that one should say beforehand: 'They
> will not believe you.' [264]

In his translation of this fragment, Schickedanz adds
the following note:

> It is true that the great Saint-Martin was exposed to
> enormous misunderstandings. Because of his brilliant work,
> **Des erreurs et de la vérité**, he was treated by one famous
> school as a Jesuit in disguise, and the supreme principle,
> mentioned so often in his book, was regarded as the
> general of the Jesuits. [265]

However, Saint-Martin always remains optimistic:

> My task in this world has been to lead the mind of man
> by a natural way to supernatural things which belong
> to him by right, but of which he totally lost the idea
> either through his own degradation or by the instruction,
> so often false, of his teachers. This task is new, but
> it is full of numerous obstacles; and it goes so slowly
> that only after my death will it produce its most beautiful
> fruit. But it is so vast and so certain that I must greatly
> thank providence for apparently charging me with this
> task, which up until now I have seen no one fulfill, since
> those who have taught and who still teach do so only
> by demanding dutiful acceptance by recounting wonderful
> facts. [266]

At the end of numerous reflections on his own mission,
he finds a certain consolation in a striking image which seems
to him to illustrate this double role of being at once the beacon
of a new inspiration and the Unknown in the milieu of a hostile
world: the image of the dark-lantern:

> I have been generally regarded as enlightened (illuminé)
> without the world knowing, however, what this word
> really means. When I am charged with this, I reply that
> it is true, but that I am enlightened in a rare way, for
> I can, when it pleases me, make myself, like a dark-lantern,
> so that I could be close to someone for thirty years
> without him being aware of my light if he did not appear
> to me to be made in order that I should speak to him
> of it; and how few there are of that number! [267]

The interpretation which declares him on one hand a champion in the struggle against materialism, and on the other the protagonist of a strict biblicism, an interpretation which gained him innumerable readers in Germany, also calls upon the author's testimony:

> All my writings have proved that we can have confidence
> in our doctrines only so far as we have placed our spirit
> in the tutelage of Holy Scripture. One exception is my
> first work, entitled **Des erreurs et de la vérité**, because
> in this work, my only goal being to protest materialistic
> philosophy, I was unable to reveal the end towards which
> I was leading the reader without exposing him to the
> danger of being disillusioned in advance, the Scriptures
> are in such discredit among men. [268]

The consciousness of his divine mission and the consciousness of having his foundation in evangelical revelation gave him the conviction that he had to persevere through all the afflictions of his life:

> My work has its base and its course in the divine. That
> is why it is such a stranger to sensibility and so little
> noticed by the outside world. It will, I hope, also come
> to its termination in this same divinity. That is why it
> will be done freely, delightfully, and completely only
> when I have freed myself from these earthly trappings.
> This world is unable to receive and accept the work
> of a man of peace who wishes only to live and act
> in principle. So my interruptions, my deprivations, even
> my tribulations do not alarm me, although they injure
> me and make me suffer and weep. I sense that in the
> midst of all this gloomy, dark distress, a secret thread
> holds me to keep me safe; I believe I am like a man
> who has fallen into the sea, but who holds in his hand
> a line which is firmly wrapped around his wrists and
> which is joined to the ship. Despite the fact that he
> is the plaything of the waves, despite the fact that the
> billows submerge him and flow over his head, they cannot
> swallow him up; from time to time he feels his life-line

and has the firm hope that he will soon be back aboard ship. [269]

Thus, there is evidently in Saint-Martin a certain correspondence between his own conception of his work and the interpretation the German circles gave it. It seems to me the idealistic and romantic interpretation, especially Franz von Baader's, corresponds exactly to the genius of the Unknown Philosopher and that his German interpreters have acquired the right to claim for themselves less the role of the cemetery, where none of the corpses hear the Unknown Philosopher' violin, than the role of the "ship," which transported him from his state of isolation to a less hostile island, if we exclude a few snakes in the intellectual wood-pile, snakes which seem to belong inevitably to biographies of philosophers and even more to those of theosophers.

NOTES

1. Eugène Susini, **Franz von Baader et le romantisme mystique,** tome I: **Baader et son temps,** in prep.; II and III: **La philosophie de Franz von Baader.** Paris: Librairie philosophique J. Vrin, 1942; t. IV: **La philosophie social et politique de Franz von Baader,** in prep. By the same author: **Lettres inédites de Franz von Baader,** Bibliothèque d'Histoire de la Philosophie, t. I, Paris, librairie philosophique J. Vrin, 1942; t. II, **notes and commentaries,** Wien, Herder, 1951; t. III, **notes and commentaries,** Wien, Herder, 1951; t. IV. Paris Presses Universitaires de France. 1967.

2. Letter to Dr. v. Stransky, Munich, Jan. 26, 1813, see Franz von Baader, **Sämmtl. Werke,** hgg. von Fr. Hoffmann, Bd. 15, Brief nr. 34, p. 250. The "certain man" was H. von Spaun.

3. The fiercest attack against mysticism on the part of Protestant theology came from Prof. Emil Brunner, **Die Mystik und Das Wort, Der Gegensatz zwischen moderner Religionsauffassung und christlichem Glauben, dargestellt an der Theologie Schleiermachers,** Tübingen, 1924. To be convinced of the legitimacy of Christian mysticism, he had to spend two years in Japan and encounter the Japanese mysticism represented by Uchimura, founder of the no-church-movement (mu-kyo-kai).

4. See Wilhelm Lütgert, **Die Religion des deutschen Idealismus und ihr Ende,** Bd. II. Gütersloh, 1923, p. 137.

5. H. Martensen, **Meister Eckhart.** Hamburg, 1842.

6. Franz Pfeiffer, **Deutsche Mystiker des 14. Jahrhundert,** Bd. I, 1835, p. ix.

7. Wilhelm Dilthey, especially in his work: **Auffassung und Analyse des Menschen im 15. und 16. Jahrhundert; Der etwicklungsgeschichtliche Pantheismus nach seinem geschichtlichen Zusammenhang mit den alteren pantheistischen Systemen,** Ges. Schriften, Bd. 2, 2. Aufl. 1921, especially pp. 55, 58, 312, 314, 320, 348; more detailed biographical notes on this theme in Ernst von Bracken, **Meister Eckhart and Fichte.** Würzburg, 1943, especially p. 582.

8. Heinrich Maier, **Philosophie der Wirklichkeit,** Bd. III, **Die psychisch-geistige Wirklichkeit,** hgg. von Anneliese Maier, Tübingen, 1935, p. 84-95. Heinz Heimsöth speaks in his famous book, **Die sechs grossen Themen der abendländischen Metaphysik** of the "vielfach gleichsam unterirdischen Verlaufe," of the Eckhartian tradition in the history of metaphysics up to the time of Fichte, Schelling, and

Hegel and regrets that the coherence of this tradition has never been studied (2. Aufl. 1934, p. 35). Special studies are found in Robert Schneider's lost book, **Schellings und Hegels schwabische Geistesahnen.** Würzburg, 1938. Most of the copies of this book were burnt by the bombing of Würzburg during the war; the author himself was killed; thus the work has remained almost unknown. The most important contribution from the side of Protestant theology for the study of our theme was Wilhelm Lütgert's work, **Die Religion des deutschen Idealismus und ihr Ende,** Bd. 1-4, Gütersloh, 1923; see also Fritz Leese, **Von Jakob Boehme zu Schelling. Zur Metaphysik des Gottesproblems,** 1927; Fritz Leese, **Philosophie und Theologie im Spätidealismus, Forschungen zur Auseinandersetzung von Christentum und idealistischer Philosophie im 19. Jahrhundert,** 1919; Emanuel Hirsch, **Die idealistische Philosophie und das Christentum,** 1926; Erich Seeberg, "Krisis der Kirche und des Christentums heute," in **Sammlung gemeinverständlicher Vorträge,** Tübingen, 1939, p. 13ff.; Erich Seeberg, **Meister Eckhart,** 1934; Erich Seeberg, "Meister Eckhart und Luther" in **Talwelt,** Jg. 12, 1936, p. 3ff.; Erich Seeberg, **Menschwerdung und Geschichte,** Stuttgart, 1943.

9. Gottfried Fischer, **Geschichte der Entdeckung der deutschen Mystiker, Eckhart, Tauler u. Seuse im 19. Jahrhundert.** Freiberg i. U., 1931; Julius Hamberger's article is still surprisingly current today: "Meister Eckhart, der Vater der deutschen Spekulation." It is to be found in his book: **Christentum und moderne Cultur,** NF, Erlanger, 1867, Abh. III, pp. 14-25. This article is a critique of Josef Bach's book: **Meister Eckhart der Vater der deutschen Spekulation. Ein Beitrag zu einer Geschichte der deutschen Theologie und Philosophie der mittleren Zeit.** Wien, 1864.

10. Franz von Baader, **Sämmtl. Werke,** Bd. 14, p. 93: "Meister Eckhart, der erleuchtetste aller Theologen des Mittelalters."

11. Franz von Baader, **Sämmtl. Werke,** Bd. 15, p. 159. Baader liest St. Martin, Meister Eckhart, Tauler 1823 in Berlin nach seiner Rückkehr aus dem Baltikum am 23. Nov. 1823. In Berlin hielt er sich acht Monate auf. Varnhagen äussert sich über jenen Berliner Aufenthalt Baaders (Classen, p. 67f.): "Da er keine Bücher mit sich führte, so entlieh er deren vom mir, vor allem Tauler, Eckhart, St. Martin, die ich alle wiederbekam mit vielen Spuren seiner zahlreichen Bemerkungen, die er mit seinem Bleistift fast auf jeder Seite beigeschrieben, nachher aber wieder ausgelöscht hatte . . . Wissenschaftlichen Umgang hatte er besonders mit Hegel unter beiderseitiger starker Anziehung; dann mit Markheineke, mit dem er aus früherer Zeit näher bekannt war; mit dem Geh. Rat Johannes Schuler; ferner besuchte er den Buchhändler Georg Reimer, dem seine kleinen Schriften, **Fermenta cognitionis** genannt, verlegte und auch einigemal Schleiermacher, der ihn aber wenig befriedigte, und dessen Standpunkt er mit Hegel und Marheineke für einen überwundenen erklärte."

12. In his works, Baader was constantly preoccupied with working out a synthesis between Eckhart and Jacob Boehme.

13. Franz von Baader, **Sämmtl. Werke,** Bd. 5, p. 263.

14. Franz von Baader, "Einleitung in die Vorlesungen über spekulative Dogmatik," **Sämmtl. Werke,** Bd. 8, p. 300f.

15. Franz von Baader, **Sämmtl, Werke,** Bd. 8, p. 199. ("Vorlesung über spekulative Dogmatik" Heft 2).

16. Franz von Baader, **Sämmtl. Werke,** Bd. 9, p. 37. ("Vorlesung über spekulative Dogmatik" Heft 5); see also Bd. 4, p. 314; Bd. 5, p. 272; Bd. 8, pp. 199, 291, 300.

17. Georg Wilh. Fr. Hegel, "Vorlesungen über die Philosophie der Religion," Bd. 1, **Sämmtl. Werke,** hgg. von Hermann Glockner, Bd. XV, p. 228.

18. I recall this expression from his lecture to Eranos at Ascona in August, 1954 on **La colombe et la ténèbre dans la mystique byzantine ancienne,** published in the **Eranos–Jahrbuch,** Bd. XXIII, p. 388ff.

19. Gustav Schnürer, **Kirche und Kultur im Mittelalter,** Bd. III, Paderborn, 1929, p. 174: "Nachdem die Dominkaner sich eine zeitlang wenig um ihre Frauenklöster gekümmert hatten, waren zwischen 1286 und 1290 die Ordensprofessoren ausdrücklich von ihrem deutschen Provinzial angewiesen worden, sich um die Betreuung ihrer Schwestern zu sorgen. Besonders in Strassburg hatte Eckhart Gelegenheit, dieser Weisung nachzukommen, denn es gab damals dort nicht weniger als 7 Frauenklöster des Dominikanerordens."

20. Meister Eckhart **Lateinische Werke,** Bd. IV, **Sermones,** ed. and translated by Ernst Benz, Bruno Decker, and Joseph Koch, Stuttgart, 1956.

21. Joseph Koch in the introduction to the Latin sermons, Bd. IV, p. xxx: "Wir stehen in Eckharts Werkstatt und können alle Stadien seiner Arbeit von einer kurzen Skizze oder aneinander gereihten Notizen bis zur formgerechten Predigt verfolgen . . . Die Entwürfe haben keine endgültige Redaktion erfahren und sind nicht aufeinander abgestimmt . . . "

22. See the details in Joseph Quint's work **Die Überlieferung der deutschen Predigten Meister Eckharts,** Bonn, 1932.

23. See Augustinus Daniels, "Eine lateinische Rechtfertigungsschrift des Meister Eckhart" in **Beiträge zur Geschichte der Philosophie des Mittelalters,** Bd. XXXIII, Heft 5, 1923, and Gabriel Théry, "Edition critique des pièces relatives au procès d'Eckhart contenues dans la manuscrit 33b de la bibliothèque de Soest," **Archives d'Histoire Doctrinale et littéraire du Moyen Age,** I, 1926, pp. 129–168.

24. On Master Eckhart's philosophical terminology, see Theophora Schneider, **Der intellektuelle Wortschatz Meister Eckeharts. Ein Beitrag zur Geschichte des deutschen Sprachinhalts,** Berlin, 1935; Benno Scholdt, **Die deutsche Begriffssprache Meister Eckharts. Studien zur philosophischen Terminologie des Mittelhochdeutschen,** Heidelberg, 1954; Rudolf Fahrner, "Wortsinn und Wortschöpfung bei Master Eckhart" in **Beiträge zur deutschen Literaturwissenschaft,** ed. by Ernst Elster, Nr. 31, Marburg, 1929.

25. This story has yet to be written. The bibliographical base of the story was given by Werner Buddecke, **Die Jakob Boehme-Ausgaben, Ein beschreib-**

endes Verzeichnis, 2. Teil: the translation in **Arbeiten aus der Staats--und Uni-versitäts--bibliotek Göttingen, Neue Folge** Bd. 2, Göttingen 1955. The list of Latin, Dutch, English and Welsh, French, Italian, Danish, Norwegian, Swedish, Finnish, and Russian translations comprises 267 pages! Besides the French translations by Saint-Martin there is another, **Le Chemin pour aller à Christ**, pub. by Gotthard Schlecht-iger, Imprimeur du Roi et de la Soc. des Sciences, 1722, of which the anonymous author is of French Huguenot origin. He writes that Boehme has returned from abroad, reformed to his Lutheran native-land, where he was first accepted, "from which it follows that the Lutherans have received this gift from the hand of the Reformed. There he (God) has reunited in the readers who search God, the two Religions, and of these two has made but one in Christ (Buddecke, 181)."

26. See Ernst Benz, "Jacob Boehme als Prophet," **Abhandlungen der Akademie der wissenschaften u.d. Lit.,** Mainz, Geistes-und sozialwissenschaftl. Klasse, Jg. 1959, Nr. 3, p. 43ff.

27. 50 Theosoph. Sendbrief an Hrn. Martin Mosern zum Goldberge, 15. Mai 1624 Theos. revel., t. II, p. 3892, nr. 10: "Was mein Vaterland wegwirft, das werden fremde Völker mit Frenden aufheben." 55. Theosoph, Sendbrief, April 3, 1624, Theos. revel., t. II, p. 3099 nr. 13-14:

> Jedoch wisset, das euch mitternächtigen Ländern eine Lilie blühet. So ihr dieselbe mit dem sektirischen Zanke der Gelehrten nicht werdet zerstören/so wird sie zum grossen Baume bei euch werden. Werdet ihr aber lieber wollen zanken, als den wahren Gott erkennen, so gehet der Strahl vorüber/und trift nur etliche; so müsset ihr hernach Wasser für den Durst eurer Seelen bey fremden Völkern holen.
>
> nr. 17: "Es gaffe Niemand mehr nach der Zeit/sie ist schon geboren. Wens trifft den triffts; wer da wachet der sihet/und der da schläffet/der sihets nicht."

28. On the "Lilienzeit" see Theos. revel., t. II, p. 2970 nr. 10; p. 3727 nr. 12 (Theosoph. Sendbrief nr. 5 an Carl von Endern): "Aber unterdessen grünet die Linie im Wunder, wider welche der letzte Antichrist Verfolgung erräget/da dan sein Ende kommt; dan die Erscheinung des Herrn erstickt ihn . . . doch werden meine Schriften zur selben Zeit wol dienen: Dan es kommt eine Zeit vom Herrn/ die nicht aus dem gestirnten Himmel ist." Baader means in his essay on "Das Blitz als Vater des Lichts," 1815, that the "time of lilies" of which Boehme speaks so often and in which he prophesies that his own works will be welcomed and re-spected, "without doubt would have already happened," especially in regard to the "revelation of Natural Magic or man's immediate and original domination over nature." (Letter to Meyer, Dec. 4, 1815).

29. Karl Robert Popp, **Jakob Boehme und Isaak Newton,** Leipzig, 1035; Edgar Edenheimer, **Jakob Boehme und die Romantiker,** Heidelberg, 1904; H. Martensen, **Jakob Boehme,** Kopenhagen, 1881 (Danish); W. Struck, **Der Einfluss Jakob Boehme auf die englische Literatur des 17. Jahrhunderts,** Berlin, 1936; Nils Thune, **The Boehmenists and the Philadelphians, A Contribution to the Study of English Mysticism**

in the 17th and 18th Centuries. Uppsala, 1948; C. Walton, To the Christianity of
the Age, London, 1854 (on Boehme in England); E. S. Haldane, "Jacob Boehme
and his Relation to Hegel" in The Philosophical Review, 1897.

30. On the rediscovery of Jacob Boehme by Oetinger see Ernest Benz,
Swedenborg in Deutschland, F. C. Oetingers und Immanuel Kants Auseinandersetzung
mit der Person und Lehre Emanuel Swedenborgs, nach neuen Quellen bearbeitet,
Frankfort am Main, 1948; cf. F. C. Oetinger, Inbegriff der Grundweisheit oder kurzer
Auszug aus den Schriften des teutschen Philosophen in einem verständlicheren
Zusammenhang; see c. I: Kurzer Aufriss der Hauptlehren Jacob Böhms, 1774. By
the same F. C. Oetinger, Versuch einer Auflössung der 177 Fragen aus Jacob Boehme,
1777, livre attaché à Halatophili Irenaei Vorstellung, wie viel Jacob Böhme's Schriften
zur lebendigen Erkenntnis beitragen. Oetinger adds there an "Anhang. Cautelen
und Vorschläge der Vorsichtigkeit in Bestrebung nach der Prophetia oder geheimer
Kenntnisse und Lesung der Bücher, die näher von der Quelle des Geistes Gottes
als andere entsprungen zu sein scheinen": see also, F. C. Oetinger, Sämmtl. Schriften,
hgg. von Karl C. E. Ehmann, 2. Abth, I. Bd., pp. 247-392 and "Anhang, wie man
Jakob Böhme mit Vorsicht lesen soll." pp. 392-396.

31. Susini writes on the subject of the Strasbourg milieu through whom
Saint-Martin was introduced to Jacob Boehme's work:

> Among those in Strasbourg who held a place in the theoso-
> pher's heart and who made him decide to learn German
> in order to read Jacob Boehme, Matter mentions Rodolphe
> Salzmann, Mme. de Boecklin (Saint-Martin's favorite who
> called him 'my B'), Major de Meyer, Baron de Ratzenreid,
> Mme. de. Westermann, and a lady (whom Saint-Martin
> designated only by the street on which she lived), whose
> real name was Mlle. Schwing, who figures in the correspon-
> dence between Mme. de Boecklin and the Baroness de
> Ratzenreid, cf. Matter, Louis Claude de Saint-Martin,"
> p. 156. (Franz von Baader, Lettres inédites, t. III, Wien,
> 1951, p. 463).

32. St. Martin, Le ministère de l'homme-esprit, Paris, 1802, p. 43;
cf. Oeuvres posthumes, t. I, p. 65:

> It seems to me that I could learn but not teach; it seems
> to me that I was in a state of discipleship and not a
> master. But, except for my first teacher, Martinez de
> Pasqually, and my second teacher, Jacob Boehme, dead
> these one hundred and fifty years, I have seen on earth
> only men who wished to be masters but who were not
> even fit to be disciples.

33. Jacob Boehme used a great many concepts belonging to the tradition
of Paracelsus and the cabala, but giving them a completely new meaning; and
he also created many arbitrary and sometimes very strange new concepts, especially
with the aid of a most unsophisticated etymology; his style was very difficult
even for his contemporaries to understand; because of his somber and mystical

108

quality and his ambiguity, he presents a sharp contrast with the clarity of the French language; evidently it was a most difficult task to translate his work into French.

34. On Jacob Boehme in Russia see D. Tschizewskij, "Deutsche Mystik in Russland" in Geistige Arbeit, Jg. 5, nr. 21, Berlin, 1938, p. 3-5, and F. Vernadskij, "Beiträge zur Geschichte der Freimaurerei und des Mystizimus in Russland" in Zeitschrift für slavische Philologie, Bd. 4, Liepzig – 1927, pp. 162-178; **Enciklopediceski Slovar**, t. 3, St. Petersburg 1890, p. 415, see the article "Bem ili Beme." On the Russian translations see W. Buddeke, 2 Teil, p. 219f. and 227f.

35. Anton Lutterbeck, **Über den Philosophischen Standpunkt Baaders**, Mainz, 1854. He writes that after the first reading of Boehme, Baader "sei so wild and unmutig geworden, das er sie vor Zorn wider die Wand warf."

36. Franz von Baader, draft of a new edition of Jacob Boehme's work, in 1828-33, **Sämmtl. Werke**, 15, pp. 446; 476ff. 491; draft of an edition of **Gnadenwahl** in 1836, **Sämmtl Werke**, 15, p. 541; of the **Mysterium Magnum, Sämmtl. Werke** 15, p. 569; draft of an edition of **Mysterium Magnum** and of **Gnadenwahl** in 1838, **Sämmtl. Werke**, 15, pp. 570-579; 655; 688. Baader's writings on Jacob Boehme: 1) "Über J. Boehmes Lehre, aus den hinterlassenen Studienbüchern," **Sämmtl. Werke**, 13, pp. 331-392; 2) "Erläuternde Anmerkungen zu J. Boehmes Abhandlung über die Gnadenwahl" (1832), **Sämmtl. Werke**, 13, pp. 237-316; 3) "Aus Privatvorlesungen über J. Boehmes Lehre mit besonderer Beziehung auf dessen Schrift von der Gnadenwahl, Sommersemester 1829," **Sämmtl. Werke**, 13, pp. 57-158; 4) "Vorlesungen über die Lehre J. Boehmes, mit besonderer Beziehung auf dessen Schrift Mysterium Magnum (Winter u. Frühling 1833)," **Sämmtl. Werke**, 13, pp. 159-236. 5) Vorlesungen über J. Boehmes Theologumena und Philosopheme, **Sämmtl. Werke**, 3, pp. 357-432; 6) Bruchstück eines Commentars zu J. Boehmes Abhandlung über die Gnadenwahl (1835), **Sämmtl. Werke**, 13, pp. 237-316. Boehme is cited in Baader under the title "der Reformator der Religionswissenschaft," **Sämmtl. Werke**, 2, p. 199; "der Stifter der wahrhaft deutschen Physiosophie und Theosophie," **Sämmtl. Werke**, 9, p. 304; "ein Mann nicht der Vergangenheit, sondern der Gegenwart und der Zukunft," **Sämmtl. Werke**, 15, p. 572.

37. Franz von Baader, **Sämmtl. Werke**, Bd. 15, p. 381, Brief nr. 104 an Varnhagen von Ense, Schwabing 30. avril 1822.

38. Franz von Baader, **Sämmtl. Werke**, Bd. 2, p. 199 (**Einleitung in die Fermenta cognitionis**, Heft 2, Berlin 1822). His lectures on Jacob Boehme are published in **Sämmtliche Werke**, Bd. 3 and 13.

39. Franz von Baader, **Sämmtl. Werke**, Bd. 15, p. 280; Brief nr. 56 an Major von Meyer, Schwabing 4. Dec. 1815. He adds the following words: "und besonders wird nun bei uns wahr, was J. Boehme in **Mysterium Magnum** c. 41 § 39 sagt von der Notwendigkeit des Wiederoffenbarwerdens der Magia naturalis."

40. Hegel's Dutch friend, P. G. van Ghert, offered his teacher an edition of the complete works of Jacob Boehme, two folio volumes (**Theosophia revelata**, II Vol. Amsterdam 1715, ed. by J. W. Überfeld). See Hegel, **Briefe**, Bd. 1, p. 317,

letter from Amsterdam, June 22, 1810, and the second offer in a letter from Amsterdam Sept. 21, 1810. Hegel replied from Nürnberg, Oct. 25, 1810:

> Ihr schönes Geschenk der Folioausgabe von J. Boehmes Schriften nehme ich mit dem herzlichsten Danke an; ich hatte schon lange gewünscht, in den Besitz der ganzen Sammlung seiner Werke zu kommen; es freut mich doppelt, eine so vorzügliche Ausgabe und sie von Ihrer Güte zu erhalten.

In May 1811, the two volumes arrived at Hegel's house. In his **Haushaltungsbuch,** the following notes are found:

> 21. Mai 1811 Fingerhut für Marie I f. für 12 Halsbinden 12 f. Accisbrief Amsterdam wegen Böhms Werken 36 c. 4. Juli. 4f. 47 c Fracht und Spe(sen) des J. Böhms (Werke) von Amsterdam.

From Nürnberg, July 29, 1811, Hegel replied to his friend, van Ghert:

> Ich kann Jakob Boehme nun genauer studieren als vorher, weil ich nicht selbst im Besitz seiner Schriften war; seine Theosophie ist immer einer der merkwürdigsten Versuche eines tiefen, jedoch ungebildeten Menschen, die innerste Natur des absoluten Wesens zu erfassen.--Für Deutschland hat er das besondere Interesse, dass er eigentlich der erste deutsche Philosoph ist.--Bei der wenigen Fähigkeit seiner Zeit und bei seiner eigenen wenigen Bildung, abstrakt zu denken ist sein Bestreben der härteste Kampf, das tiefe Spekulative, das er in seiner Anschauung hat, in die Vorstellung zu bringen, und zugleich das Element des Vorstellens so zu bewältigen, dass das Spekulative darin gedruckt werden könnte.

We find the reflections of this rediscovery of Boehme in the following works: Ch. H. Weisse, **Das philosophische Problem der Gegenwart, Sendsschreiben an J. H. Fichte,** Leipzig 1842, pp. 250-251; and D. J. Hamberger, **Die Lehre des deutschen Philosophen Jacob Boehme,** Munich in 1844. Hoffmann, "Einleitung zum I. Band der Gesammtausgabe der Werke Franz von Baaders," p. LXI writes on Weisse:

> Auch Weisse, der von der Persönlichkeit Boehmes eine ergreifende Schliderung gegeben hat (Fichte's Zeitschrift für Philosophie und spekulative Theologie XIV, pp. 136ff.) spricht nur mit Bewunderung von den urgewaltigen, riesenhaften Anschauungen dieses herrlichen Geistes und genialen Denkers und findet in der kecken Berufung des modernen Pantheismus auf diesen theistischen Forscher ein Zeichen der Zeit, dass die ächte Anerkennung dieses hohen Geists und seines wahren Gedankeninhaltes nicht mehr fern sei.

Baader intended to dedicate the edition of **Mysterium Magnum,** by J. Boehme, which he prepared, to Hegel. On Sept. 20, 1830, he wrote to him from Munich:

110

". . . and mache Eur. Hoch. bei dieser Gelegenheit die vorläufige Anzeige, dass meine nächste Schrift (**Vorlesungen über J. Böhms Mysterium Magnum**) Ihnen dediziert, binnen 2 oder 3 Monaten erscheinen wird" (Briefe Krit. Ausgabe Bd. III, nr. 648, p. 312). These lectures were published by Hoffmann only after the death of Baader in **Sämmtliche Werke**, Bd. XIII, pp. 159-236.

41. On Pregizer there is now an excellent monograph by Gotthold Müller, **Christian Gottlob Pregizer, Sein Leben und seine Schriften**, Stuttgart 1961.

42. See Ernst Benz, "Schellings theologische Geistesahnen." **Abhndl. d. Akad. d. Wiss. u. d. Lit.** Mainz, Geistes-u. soz. wiss. Klasse. Jg. 1955, nr. 3, p. 36; cf. Plitt, **Schellings Leben in Briefen**, Bd. 11, p. 252f.

42a. Papus (= Dr. G. Encausse), **Martinésisme, Willermozisme et Franc-maçonnerie**, Paris 1899; A. E. Waite, **St. Martin, The French Mystic and the Story of Modern Martinisme**, London 1922; F. Schneider, **Die Freimaurerei und ihre Einflüsse auf die geistige Kultur in Deutschland am Ende des 18. Jahrhunderts**, Prague 1919; R. Le Forestier, **Les Illuminés de Bavière et la Franc-maçonnerie Allemande**, Paris 1815, Jacques Roos, **Aspects littéraires du mysticisme philosophique et l'influence de Boehme et de Swedenborg au début du romantisme: William Blake, Novalis, Ballanche**, Strasbourg, P. H. Heitz, 1951.

43. See Ernst Benz, **Swedenborg in Deutschland**, Frankfurt a. M., 1948, with unpublished documents.

44. To these dramas belong also the frequent attempts made among friends to appear to the survivor after death by predetermined signs, as, for example, Lavater and Hesse; see Ernst Benz, "Swedenborg und Lavater, Über die religiösen Grundlagen der Physiognomik" in Zeitschrift für Kirchengeschichte, Dritte Folge VIII, Bd. LVIII, 1938, Heft 1-2, pp. 153-216.

45. On Karoline, see B. Zade, **Karoline Schelling**, Stockholm 1914; M. Schauer, **Caroline Schlegel-Schelling**, 1922; G. Mielke, **Caroline Schelling nach ihren Briefen**, Diss. Greifswald 1925; Margarete Susman, **Frauen der Romantik**, 1929; A. Apt, **Caroline und die frühromantische Gesellschaft**, Diss. Königsburg 1926; Th. Düring, **Caroline**, 1942; **Briefe aus der Frühromantik**, hgg. von G. Waitz, 2 Bde 1871, vermehrt von E. Schmidt, 2 Bde 1914.

46. See Ernst Benz, "Swedenborg als geistiger Wegbahner des deutschen Idealismus und der deutschen Romantik" in Deutsche Vierteljahrsschrift für Literaturwissenschaft und Geistesgeschichte, Jg. XIX, Heft 1, pp. 1-32; Friedemann Horn, **Swedenborg und Schelling, Ein Beitrag zur Problemgeschichte des deutschen Idealismus**, Lorrach 1954.

47. **Schelling Leben in Briefen**, hgg. von. G. I. Plitt, Leipzig 1970, Bd. 11, 1803-1820, p. 252.

48. H. de Lubac, "La rencontre du Bouddhisme et de l'Occident" in Théologie, Etudes, publ. sous la direction de la Faculté de Théologie S. J. de Lyon-Fourvière, nr. 24, Paris 1952.

49. On this theme there is an excellent, rarely used work by Ludwig Alsdorf, **Deutsch indische Geistesbeziehungen,** Heidelberg-Berlin-Magdeburg, Vohwinckel 1942, in the series **Indien,** ed. by Vohwinckel, Vol. 7. Other studies: Paul Theodor Hoffmann, **Der indische und der deutsche Geist von Herder bis zur Romantik,** Diss., Tübingen 1915; Susanne Sommerfeld, **Indienschau und Indiendeutung romantischer Philosophen,** Zürich 1953. Helmut von Glasenapp's book, **Das Indienbild deutscher Denker,** was published in Stuttgart 1960. On the encounter of Indian spirituality and German philosophy, see Wilhelm Lütgert, **Die Religion des deutschen Idealismus,** Bd. 11, p. 78ff; F. Kreis, "Hegels Interpretation der indischen Geisteswelt." Zeitschrift für deutsche Kulturphilosophie 1941, p. 133ff., and Hans-Joachim Schoeps, "Die ausserchristlichen Religionen bei Hegel." Zeitschrift für Religions-und Geistesgeschichte, Jg. VII, 1955, Heft I, c. I, 2: Indien. Along with Friedrich Schlegel's book, romantic philosophers were inspired by J. F. Goerres' work **Mythengeschichte der asiatischen Religionen.**

50. On Herder, see Helmut von Glasenapp, **Das Indienbild deutscher Denker,** pp. 14-24; Alsdorf, p. 12ff.

51. Friedrich Schlegel, **Über die Sprache und Weisheit der Inder,** Heidelberg 1808, now in **Sämmtl. Werke, Kritische Ausgabe,** Bd. 6: **Geschichte der alten und neuen Literatur,** hgg. von Hans Eichner, München-Wien 1961.

52. Novalis, **Geistliche Lieder II, Rowohlts Klassiker der Literatur und der Wissenschaft, Deutsche Literatur,** Bd. II, p. 71.

53. Cf. Hans-Joachim Schoeps, "Das Indienbild Hegels" in Zeitschrift für Religions-und Geistesgeschichte, Jg. VII, p. 5.

54. H. de Lubac, **La rencontre,** p. 128 and Wilhelm Lütgert, **Die Religion des deutschen idealismus und ihr Ende,** Bd. 11, Gütersloh 1927, p. 78.

55. Friedrich Schlegel, **Über die Sprache und Weisheit der Inder,** p. 125 (original edition of 1808).

56. Ibid., p. 207.

57. Ibid., p. 208. The same phenomenon is found in Schopenhauer, who was profoundly influenced in his interpretation of Indian philosophy, especially Buddhism, by Christian mysticism; see Jacob Bühletaler, **Die Mystik bei Schopenhauer,** Berlin 1920; his knowledge of German mystics, pp. 21-55; other European mystics, pp. 56-75.

58. See St. Martin, **Ministère de l'homme-esprit,** p. 56.

59. Franz von Baader discovered Master Eckhart and inspired Pfeiffer's edition. For Baader, Master Eckhart is "der Erleuchtetste aller Theologen des Mittelalters," **Sämmtl. Werke,** 14, p. 93.

60. On the spark of the soul in Master Eckhart, see Hans Hof, **Scintilla animae, Eine Studien zu einem Grundbegriff in Meister Eckharts Philosophe,** Lund-Bonn 1952; Shizuteru Ueda (Kyoto), **Die Gottesgeburt in der Seele und der Durchbruch zur Gottheit, Die mystische Anthropologie Meister Eckharts und ihre Konfrontation mit der Mystik des Zen-Buddhismus,** Gütersloh 1965.

61. **Maître Eckhart,** Procès, ed. G. Théry, Paris 1926, p. 179; cf. **Deutsche Werke,** Bd. I, p. 183, Anm. I (Quint); and Franz Pfeiffer, **Meister Eckhart,** Göttingen 1914, p. 207, z. 11-12, with some corrections by Quint.

62. **Paradimus animae,** hgg. von Ph. Strauch. Berlin 1919, p. 121. z. 11-15.

63. **Maître Eckhart,** Pfeiffer, p. 281, z. 20-p. 284, z. 4, according to Quint's translation, cf. Pfeiffer, p. 181, z. 3 ss.; p. 285, z. 14 ss. and the note in Ernst von Bracken, **Meister Eckhart und Fichte,** Würzburg 1943, p. 648.

64. Ernst von Bracken says in the preface of his book:

> Sein Thema ist das verwandtschaftliche Verhältnis zwischen der Philosophie des deutschen Idealismus und der Mystik oder bestimmter ausgedrückt, die Geburt des Idealismus aus dem Geiste der Mystik.

> Ibid., p. 423: "Das ich Fichtes ist mutatis mutandis der Seelenfunken M. Eckharts im Zustande voller Aktualisierung der intelligiblen Erkenntnis."

The idea of mystical union is found again in Fichte as the central idea of his religious philosophy. See Joh. Gottl. Fichte, "Anweisung sum seligen Leben," **Sämmtl. Werke,** hgg. von J. H. Fichte, Bd. V. Leipzig, s. a. II. Abth. Bd. 111, p. 407 on the "Sehnsucht nach dem Ewigen": "Dieser Trieb, mit dem Unvergänglichen vereinigt zu werden und zu verschmelzen, ist die innigste Wurzel alles endlichen Daseyns, und ist in keinem Zweige dieses Daseyns ganz auszutilgen, falls nicht dieser Zweig versinken soll in völliges Nichtseyn."

65. Franz von Baader, **Sämmtl. Werke,** Bd. 12, p. 346.

65a. Franz von Baader, **Sämmtl. Werke,** Bd. 2, p. 354 (**Fermenta cognitionis,** Heft 4, 1824), p. 354 . . .

65b. Franz von Baader, **Sämmtl. Werke,** Bd. 15, p. 427, Brief nr. 140 an Emilie Linder, München, 25, mai 1825; cf. Hegel on "Boehme Vorlesungen über die Philosophie der Religion," Bd. 11, **Sämmtl. Werke,** hgg. von H. Glockner, Stuttgart 1959, Bd. 16. 246 im Dritten Theil: "Die absolute Religion, Das Reich des Vaters":

> Dem Jakob Böhm ist diess Geheimniss der Dreifaltigkeit auf eine andere Weise aufgegangen. Die Weise seines Vorstellens, seines Denkens ist allerdings mehr phantastisch und wild; er hat sich nicht erhoben in reine Formen des Denkens, aber diess ist die herrschende Gründlichkeit seins Gährens und Kämpfens gewesen, die Dreieinigkeit

113

in Allem, überall zu erkennen, z.B. "Sie muss im Herzen des Menschen geboren werden." Sie ist die allgemeine Grundlage von Allem, was nach der Wahrheit betrachtet wird, zwar als Endliches aber in seiner Endlichkeit als die Wahrheit, die in ihm ist. So hat Jakob Böhm die Natur und das Herz, den Geist des Menschen in dieser Bestimmung sich Vorstellung zu machen versucht.

The same transposition of the trinitarian life into the soul is found in **Vorlesungen über die Geschichte der Philosophe,** Bd. 19, p. 323: "Die Geburt der heiligen Dreifaltigkeit geschieht auch in deinem herzen; es werden alle drei Personen in deinem Herzen geboren, Gott Vater, Sohn, und Heiliger Geist."

66. **Die Anweisung zum seligen Leben, gehalten zu Berlin 1806,** hgg. von H. Scholz, Berlin 1912 **(Deutsche Bibliothek).**

67. See Reich Gottes, Vollendung der Zeiten, Jüngstes Gericht, Ende der Zeit, in **Hegellexikon** and in the index of Baader's **Sämmtl. Werke,** hgg. von F. Hoffmann (Bd. 16, Sach-und Namenregister édité par Dr. Anton Lutterbeck, Leipzig 1860). Glockner in his **Hegel-Lexikon,** did not mention these theological terms; but they are frequently found in Hegel, for example, in the **Vorlesungen über die Philosophie der Religion II,** Bd. 16, p. 328: "Das Subjekt soll Bürger des Reiches Gottes sein."

68. On the eschatological elements in Marxism, see especially Jean-Yves Calvez's great work, **La pensée de Karl Marx,** Collections "Esprit," ed. by Seuil 1956; (ed. Allemande: Karl Marx, Darstellung und Kritik seines Denkens, Walter-Verlag Olten-Freiburg i. Br. 1964). See also Nicolas Berdiaeff, **Le christianisme et la lutte des classes,** ed. Je Sers, Paris 1932; also **Le marxisme et la religion,** ed. Je Sers, Paris 1932; and **Au seuil d'une nouvelle époque,** Delachaux, Paris 1947; Henri Chambre, "Signification philosophique et theologique du marxisme" in **Chronique Sociale de France,** 1952, nr. 4; Alexandre Koyré, "Hegel, Marx et le christianisme" in **Critique,** nrr. 3-4; Karl Loewith, **Von Hegel bis Nietzche,** Europa-Verlag, Zürich 1947; Henri de Lubac, **Le drame de l'humanisme athée,** Spes, Paris 1945; (Anon.) **Le communisme et les chrétiens,** Plon, Paris 1946; "Marxisme ouvert contre marxisme scholastique," special ed. of the review Esprit XVI, 1948 (mai-juin): especially the articles there by W. Dirks, "Le marxisme dans une vision chrétienne," and H. C. Desroches, "Théologie et marxisme." Cf. also the following works: Jakob Taubes, **Abendländische Eschatologie,** Bern 1947; Henri Chambre, **Le communisme et les chrétiens,** Paris 1946; Lucien Goldmann, **Matérialisme dialectique et histoire de la philosophie,** Paris 1947; Marcel Reding, **Der politische Atheismus,** Köln 1957.

69. Schelling, **Münchener Jubiläumsausgabe,** Bd. V, p. 286f.; cf. Robert Schneider, **Geistesahnen,** p. 149.

70. Schelling, Bd. V, p. 287.

71. Hegel, **The Phenomenology of Spirit,** Tr. by A. V. Miller, Oxford, 1977, p. 11.

72. Ibid., pp. 487–488.

73. Ibid., p. 492.

74. Robert Minder, lectures on the Swabian fathers at the College of France, 1958-59. (cf. **Annuaire du Collège de France** 1958-59); "Hegel et les pères Souabes," Etudes germaniques, déc. 1951; "Schiller et les pères Souabes, ibid., mars. 1955. On the Stift, cf. W. Betzendörfer, **Hölderlins Studienjahre im Tübinger Stift**, Heilbronn 1922; J. Klaiber, "Hölderlin, Hegel und Schelling in ihren schwäbischen Jugendjahren" in **Festschrift zur Jubelfeier der Universität Tübingen**, Stuttgart 1877; Gustav Emil Müller, **Hegel, Denkgeschichte eines Lebendigen**, Bern-München 1959, p. 35ff.: Student in Tübingen, Ernst Benz, "Schwäbische Giganto-machie, Schelling, Hegel, Paulus" in **Schelling, Werden und Wirken seines Denkens**, Zürich-Stuttgart 1955, p. 57; Kuno Fischer, **Schelling Leben, Werke und Lehre**, 4. Aufl. Heidelberg 1923, p. 9ff.

75. On Bengel, see J. C. F. Burk, **Joh. Albr. Bengels Leben und Wirken, meist nach handschriftlichen Materialien bearbeitet**, Stuttgart 1831; Oskar Wächter, **Joh. Albr. Bengel, Lebensabriss, Charakter, Briefe und Aussprüche**, Stuttgart 1865; Karl Hermann, **Joh. Albr. Bengel**, Stuttgart 1937; E. Müller, **Stiftsköpfe**, 1938, p. 145ff.; **Joh. Albr. Bengel, Erklärte Offenbarung Johannis oder vielmehr Jesu Christi**, 1740, new ed. by Wilhelm Hoffmann, Stuttgart 1834; **Sechzig erbauliche Reden über die Offenbarung Johannis oder vielmehr Jesu Christi**, 1746, new ed. Stuttgart 1870.

76. M. Leube, **Geschichte des Tübinger Stifts**, Bd. I & III, 1926-36, Bd. III, 1954, 2nd ed; Ernst Benz, "Schelling, Werden und Wirken seines Denkens," Zürich-Stuttgart 1955, in **Albae Vigilae**, ed. K. Kerenyi, N.F. Heft XV.

77. H. Fuhrmans, "Schellings Philosophie der Weltalter," 1954: Dokumente zur Schellingforschung in Kantstudien Jg. 47, 1955-56, pp. 182-91; 273-87; 378-96.

78. At Frommann-Verlag, Stuttgart.

79. The Apocalypse of St. John is taken by Bengel as the basis for an eschatological interpretation of the events of the political, literary, philosophical and religious life of his time.

80. J. C. F. Burk, **Bengels Leben,** p. 233.

81. "Gedanken von der Errichtung eines Compendii Theologiae § 4" in Oskar Wächter, p. 144; cf. Bengel's letter to Oetinger in Karl Chr. E. Ehmann; **F. C. Oetingers Leben und Briefe**, nr. 22, p. 449f.:

> Ich muss die Schrift immer mit einem Lagerbuch ver-
> gleichen, woraus ein jeder Bürger seine Pflichten und
> Gerechtsame erlernt; aber noch wichtiger ist dasjenige,
> was darin die sämmtliche Gemeinde angeht, wiewohl
> sich nicht eben ein jeder darum bekümmert . . . Gott
> führt seine Gemeinde von Anbeginn her durch das Warten

auf das Zukünftige, und zwar nicht auf das Äusserste,
sondern je and je auf das Nächst-Künftige."

82. See Ernst Benz. **Swedenborg in Deutschland,** p. 192; in the same
Rechtfertigungsschrift, ib. p. 93, the following words of Oetinger are found: "Es
ist aus denen patribus erweislich, das es von seculis zu seculis auserordentliche
Offenbarungen neben den ordentlichen gegeben; v, see also ib. pp. 174, 188, 191.

83. **Erklärte Offenbarung, Vorrede § I,** p. xiv.

84. **Sechzig erbauliche Reden,** pp. 2-4: "Die Offenbarung geht stufen-
weise, bis sie zu uns gelangt."

85. Ibid., pp. 627-28.

86. See Ernst Benz, "Johann Albrecht Bengel und die Philosophie des
deutschen Idealismus" in Deutsche Vierteljahrsschrift für Literaturwissenschaft und
Geistesgeschichte, Jg. 28, 1953, Heft 4, p. 518ff.

87. See J. C. F. Burk, **Bengels Leben,** p. 265ff., letter to his friend
J. F. Reuss on Dec. 22, 1724:

> Es ist mir unmöglich, Dir eine Nachricht vorzuenthalten,
> von der ich gleichwohl wünschen muss, dass Du sie ganz
> für dich behaltest. Unter dem Beistand des Herrn habe
> ich die Zahl des Thieres gefunden: es sind 666 Jahre
> von 1143-1809. Dieser apokalyptische Schlüssel ist von
> Wichtigkeit und tröstet mich namentlich bey den Trauer-
> Fällen meiner Familie, denn diejenigen, welche jetzt geboren
> werden, kommen in wunderbare Zeiten hinein. Auch Du
> hast Dich darauf gefasst zu machen, denn Weisheit wird
> Noth thun. Gebenedeyet sey, der da kommt."

88. Ernst Bloch attempted to interpret this phenomenon in a purely
Marxist sense in his book **Das Prinzip Hoffnung, zu fünf Teilen,** Frankfurt 1959,
by suppressing the religious sources of Christian eschatology.

89. J. F. C. Burk, **Bengels Leben,** Stuttgart 1831, p. 297.

90. Fr. Wilh. Jos. Schelling, "Die Weltalter, Fragmente, in den Urfassungen
von 1811 und 1813," hgg. M. Schroter, München 1946, in **Schellings Werke, Münchener
Jubiläumsausgabe Nachlassband.**

90a. On Johannes Coccejus and the "federal theology," see Gottlob
Schrenke, "Gottesreich und Bund im älteren Protestantismus bei Johannes Coccejus"
in **Beiträge zur Förderung christlicher Theologie,** Reihe 2, Bd. 5, Gütersloh 1923;
E. V. Korff, **Die Anfänge der Föderaltheologie und ihre erste Ausgestaltung in Zürich
und Holland,** 1908; **Religion in Geschichte und Gegenwart,** 3. Aufl., Art Bd. IV: **Foe-
deraltheologie, dogmengeschichtlich,** Bd. II, Col. 1518-20; the central work: J.
Coccejus, **Summa doctrinae de foedere et testamento dei,** 1648. The influence

116

of this "federal theology" is found again in Schelling, who wrote, for example, in his "Theologie der Offenbarung," Sämmtl. **Werke**, 2, Abth. Bd. iv, p. 333:

> "Schon die alten Theologen haben die akratos theologia, die reine Theologie, und die oikonomia unterschieden. So sagt Basilius d. G. in einem seiner Briefe: durch den heiligen Geist müsse unser Intelligenz bewahrt werden, dass wir nicht über der Theologie die Oekonomie vergessen, über der abstrakten Gotteslehre nich die geschichtliche. An diesen Hergang sind wir gewiesen . . . Die Reformation . . . wendete sich vorzüglich nach der Seite des inneren Processes . . . Den inneren Process hat jeder für sich durchzumachen; was allein gemeinsam ist, ist der Weg, der geschichtliche Hergang . . . dessen Erkenntnis allein der Kirche selbst ihre Objecktivität erhält und sie einerseits vor der Auflösung in blosse, wenn auch fromme Subjektivität, von der andern Seite vor der Auflösung ins leere Allgemeine, das bloss Rationale bewahrt.

91. **Jacobi Acontii Satanae stratagematum libri octo ad Johannem Wolphium eiusque ad Acontium spistulae**, hgg. von W. Koehler, München 1937. Recently: ed. a cura di Giorgio Badetti, Firenze 1964; in **Edizione Nazionale du Classici del Pensiero Italiana 7.**

92. Bengel, **Sechzig erbaulich Reden,** p. 395. These ideas are inspired by Luther's theology of history. See E. Seeberg, **Luthers Theologie, Motive und Ideen,** 1929; also by the same author, **Christus, Urbild und Wirklichkeit,** 1937; "Ideen zur Theologie der Geschichte" in **Menschwerdung und Geschichte,** Stuttgart, o. J. (1938?), p. 1ff., 21ff; Gunnar Hillerdal, "Luthers Geschichtsauffassung" in Studia Theologica 7, 1953, p. 28–53; Martin Schmidt, "Luthers Schau der Geschichte," Luther-Jahrbuch 1963, pp. 17–69.

93. Bengel, Sechzig erbauliche Reden, p. 460 (antigöttliche Trinität).

94. Ibid., p. 419.

95. Ibid., p. 229.

96. Hegel, **Vorrede zur Phänomenologie des Geistes,** hgg. von Lasson, **Philos. Bibl.** Bd. 114, 1921, p. 37.

97. Erich Seeberg, works cited in note 92.

98. Bengel, Op. cit., 168.

99. F. C. Oetinger, **Sämmtl. Schriften,** Bd. 6, p. 51.

100. Ibid., pp. 88, 304. Cf. Apc 1, 8; 21, 6; 2, 2, 13.

101. Ibid., p. 28.

102. Ibid., p. 20f.

103. Ibid., p. 47.

104. Ibid. p. 141.

105. Ibid., p. 300.

106. Ibid., p. 306.

107. Hegel, **Encyclopädie** § 301, Heidelberg 1817, p. 206.

108. Schelling, **Werke**, Bd. VIII, p. 305.

109. Schelling, **Nachlassband**, hgg. von Manfred Schröter, 1946, p. 83.

110. C. F. Oetinger, **Sammtl. Schriften**, Bd. 6, p. 40.

111. Bengel, **Sechzig erbauliche Reden**, p. 101.

112. Ibid., p. 270; cf. pp. 103, 225.

113. Ibid., p. 267; cf. pp. 319, 393.

114. Ernst Benz, **Schelling, werden und wirken seines Denkens**, p. 51ff.

115. See also Karl Kupisch, **Vom Pietismus zum Kommunismus**, Berlin 1953; also **Das Jahrhundert des Sozialismus und die Kirche**, Berlin 1958.

116. Oetinger, **Sammtl. Schriften**, Bd. 6, p. 29, "Jeder soll ein Freiherr sein neben dem andern."

117. Ibid., p. 29.

118. Ibid., p. 30.

119. Ibid.

120. Ibid.

121. See Ernst Benz, **Schöpfungsglaube und Endzeiterwartung, Antwort auf Teilhard de Chardins Theologie der Evolution**, München 1965.

122. See Ernst Benz, **Die christliche Kabbala, Albae Vigiliae**, N. F. Heft XVIII Zürich 1958; Eliphas Levy, **Les origines cabbalistiques du christianisme**; Gershom Scholem, **Zur Geschichte der Anfänge der christlichen Kabbala, tribute to Leo Baeck**, London 1954; J.-L. Blau, **The Christian Interpretation of the Cabala**, New York, 1944. The most important recent studies on the history of the Christian cabala are published by François Secret; note especially the following publications: 1) **Notes sur Guillaume Postel. Bibliothèque d'Humanisme et Renaissance**, t. XXVI,

pp. 453-467, t. XXII, pp. 377-392, pp. 552-565, t. XXIII, pp. 121-137, pp. 351-374, p. 524-550, t. XXV, pp. 212-222, Genève, Librairie E. Droz, 1959-1963; 2) **Guillaume Postel et les études Arabes à la Renaissance,** Arabica, t. IX, fasc. I, pp. 21-36, Leiden, Brill 1962; 3) "Les débuts du kabbalisme chrétien en Espagne et son histoire à la Renaissance," Sefarad, XVIII, 1957, pp. 36-48; 4) Pedro Ciruelo: "Critique de la kabbale et de son usage par les chrétiens." Sefarad XIX, 1959, pp. 48-77; 5) "Notes sur les hebraisants chrétiens de la Renaissance." Sefarad XXII, 1962, pp. 107-127; 6) "Notes sur Paulus Ricius et la kabbale chrétienne en Italie; Rinascimento anno XI," n. 2, 1960, pp. 169-192; 7) "L'interpretazzione della kabbala nel Rinascimento. Convivium, N.s.V. (1960), Torino, etc., pp. 541-552; 8) Pico della Mirandola e gli inizi della cabala cristiana." Convivium, N.s.I. (1957), Torino, etc., pp. 31-47; 9) "Notes sur quelques hebraisants chrétiens des XVI-XVIII siècles." Revue des études Juives, Trosième série, t. III (CXX), 1961, pp. 369-381; 10) "Les Jésuites et le Kabbalisme chrétien à la Renaissance." Bibliothèque d'Humanisme et Renaissance, t. XX, pp. 542-555, Genève, Librairie E. Droz, 1958; 11) "Le Zohar chez les kabbalistes chrétiens de la Renaissance." Mémoires de la Société des Études Juives III, 141 pp., Paris 1958. German studies on the Christian cabbala begin with J. F. Kleuker, **Über die Natur und den Ursprung der Emanationslehre bei den Kabbalisten,** Riga 1786, and are continued in German romantic philosophy by Franz Joseph Molitor in his **Philosophie der Geschichte oder über die Tradition,** I Bd. Frankfurt am Main 1827, 2nd ed. 1855; 2. Bd. Münster 1834; 3. Bd. Münster 1839; 4. Bd. Münster 1853; Julius Hamberger, **Christenthum und moderne Cultur, Kritiken und Charakterbilder nr. IX: Die Kabbalah** (1846). Erlangen 1863; **Die hohe Bedeutung der altjüdischen Tradition oder der sog. Kabbalah,** Sulzbach 1844 ("Rezension von Molitors Philosophie der Geschichte" in den **Münchener Gelehrten Anzeigen**).

123. In 1846, he published the book **Septuaginta conclusiones cabbalisticae;** see the article by François Secret on Pico, nr. 8.

124. On Reuchlin, see Ludwig Geiger, **Joh. Reuchlin, Sein Leben und seine Werke,** Leipzig 1871. Geiger considers Reuchlin's cabalistic studies as a sign of his madness. In his article, "Reuchlin," **Allgemeine Deutsche Bibliographie,** Bd. 28, p. 793, he writes of Reuchlin's cabalistic works that they can be considered today "mehr als Ausgeburt eines kranken Geistes denn als Resultate wirklich philosophischer Forchung." Also see Will-Erich Peuckert, **Pansophie,** Stuttgart 1936, pp. 113ff., 122ff.

125. The princess also seems to have worked out a theosophical interpretation of the cabalistic table. Oetinger writes of her:

> Sie stiftete eine öffentliche Tafel in dem Gesundbrunnen zu Deinach. Ihre Schriften, worin sie diese Tafel erklärt, haben sollen auf Censur des Consistoriums gedruckt werden; aber man hat es nicht der Mühe werth gehalten, diesen Dingen nachzudenken, obwohl sie die Grundweisheit der Schrift zur Theologie sehr schön zu Tage gelegt." See Ernst Benz, **Christliches Kabbala,** p. 61, note 53.

126. F. C. Oetinger, **Öffentliches Denkmal der Lehrtafel einer weil. Württembergischen Prinzessin Antonia, in Kupfer gestochen, dessen Original sie**

von den zehn Abglänzen Gottes in den Deinachischen Brunnen in einem prächtigen Gemälde gestiftet . . . hgg. von Karl C. E. Ehmann, **Oetingers Sämmtl. Schriften.** Bd. I, Stuttgart 1858.

127. See Kurt Salecker, "Christian Knorr von Rosenroth" in **Palaestra,** nr. 178, Leipzig 1931.

128. Leibniz spent ten days with von Rosenroth in Sulzbach in 1687. For his extremely favorable opinion of the baron, see Salnecker, p. 12f.

129. Ernst Benz, **Schellings theologische Geistesahnen,** p. 41f.; also **Schelling, Werden und Wirken seines Denkens,** p. 57ff.

130. Schelling, **Werke** VIII, p. 305; Ernst Benz, **Schellings theologische Geistesahnen,** pp. 50-53.

131. See Ernst Benz, **Die christliche Kabbala,** p. 31ff.; Wilhelm August Schulze, "Jacob Boehme und die Kabbala" in Judaica, Jg. 11, Heft I, 1955, p. 12ff.

132. Ernst Benz, **Schellings theologische Geistesahnen,** p. 59ff., also by the same author, **Schelling, Werden und Wirken seines Denkens,** p. 25f. Schelling **Werke** XIV, p. 207.

133. Ibid., pp. 25, and 59.

134. In the **Bayerische Annalen** 1834, nr. 28, pp. 219-24; and nr. 62, pp. 483-490, **Sämmtl. Werke,** Bd. VI, Leipzig 1854, nr. 6, p. 73ff.

135. Saint-Martin, **Oeuvres Posthumes,** Vol. I, Tours 1807, p. 42, c. 334; 73, c. 338; cf. **Ministère de l'Homme-Esprit,** p. 97ff., 146f., 164f.

136. On "essentification," see Ernst Benz, **Schellings theologische Geistes-ahnen,** p. 59; F. C. Oetinger, **Swedenborgs Ird. und Himml. Philos.,** p. 190, **Lehrtafel d. Prinz. Ant.,** p. 129f.

136a. F. C. Oetinger, **Werke,** ed. von Ehmann, Bd. II, I, p. 75; also see Wilhelm Albert Hauck, **Das Geheimnis des Lebens, Naturanschauung und Gottesauf-fassung F. C. Oetingers,** Heidelberg 1947, p. 81ff.; see the critique of idealism in C. A. Auberlen, **Die Theosophie F. C. Oetingers,** Tübingen 1867, p. 133.

137. Schelling, **Werke,** Bd. XIV, p. 205.

138. Ibid., 207.

139. F. C. Oetinger, **Bibl. Wörterbuch,** article Sabbath, p. 397.

140. F. C. Oetinger, "Abhandlung von dem Zusammenhang der Glaubens-lehren mit den letzten Dingen," **Sämmtl. Schriften,** 2. Abth., Bd. 6, p. 265.

141. Ibid., p. 464.

142. "Lehrtafel," **Sämmtl. Schriften**, 2. Abth. Bd. I, p. 129.

143. Ibid., p. 130; **Swedenborgs und anderer Irrdische und Himmlische Philosophie**, p. 190.

144. **Biblisches Wörterbuch**, ed. Hamberger, 1849, p. 139 in the article "Essen des Fleisches und Trinken des Blutes des Menschensohnes."

145. Schelling, **Werke**, Bd. XIV, p. 207.

146. Henry Corbin created this term in his studies on the idea of spiritual corporality and the resurrection body in shi'ite mysticism, especially in his last work: **Terre céleste et corps de résurrection. De l'Iran Mazdéen à l'Iran Shi'ite**, Buchet-Chastel, Korea 1960, and in **Physiologie de l'homme de lumière dans le soufisme iranien**, Paris, Desclée de Brouwer, 1960 (Académie Septentrionale, Vol. I). He emphasized the surprising resemblance between the Shi'ite idea of the celestial body and the theosophical speculations of Oetinger, especially **Terre céleste**, in the prologue, p. 14, where he wrote on the Shi'ite idea of "spiritual corporality":

> All that our writers (Shi'ites) propose here is perhaps utterly against the current of the modes of thinking of our day and may be totally misunderstood. However, we could find spiritual brothers for them among those who are called the spiritualists of Protestantism: Schwenkfeld, Boehme, the Berleburg circle, Oetinger, etc., and who also have had their perpetuators up to the present time. The term Leiblichkeit cannot be translated into French or English. In German, there is a distinction between Körper and Leib. Körper emphasizes the materialistic structure and the materialistic character; Leib contains the quality of the psychic and even spiritual structure and organization. A spirit can have a Leib, but not a Körper. In speaking of the church as the 'body of Christ' one never says in German 'der Körper Christi,' but 'der Leib Christi.'

147. Schelling, **Werke**, Bd. XIV, p. 221.

148. Ibid., Bd. VIII, p. 243.

149. Oetinger seems to have found this hermeneutical tradition in Knorr von Rosenroth, **Cabbala denudata**; see Ernst Benz, **Die christliche Kabbala c. "Knorr von Rosenroth,"** p. 18ff.

150. Schelling, **Werke**, Bd. VIII, p. 325.

151. Oetinger, **Bibl. Wörterbuch**, ed. by Hamberger with foreword by Gotthilf Heinrich Schubert, Stuttgart 1848, p. 381; cf. Schelling, **Werke**, Bd. VIII, p. 325.

152. On the indissoluble life see especially Oetinger, **Bibl. Wörterbuch,** pp. 182, 223, 294, 519; **Swedenborgs Irrdische und Himmlische Philosophie,** p. 349; Lehrtafel, pp. 117, 127, 171.

153. Schelling, **Werke,** Bd. VIII, p. 259. S. trad. S. Jankélevitch, Paris, Aubier 1949, p. 84.

154. Oetinger, **Bibl. Wörterbuch,** p. 472.

155. Oetinger, **Öffentliches Denkmal der Lehrtafel der Prinzessin Antonia,** ed. Karl Chr. E. Ehmann, Stuttgart 1858.

156. **Lehrtafel,** p. 16.

157. Ibid.

158. Ibid., p. 88.

159. Ibid., p. 133f.

160. Ibid., p. 171.

161. Ibid., pp. 16, 328, 366.

162. Oetinger, **Swedenborgs Irrdische und Himmlische Philosophie, Zur Prüfung des Besten ans Licht gestellt,** Frankfurt u. Leipzig 1765, pp. 341-345; see the chapter "Leiblichkeit" in C. A. Auberlen, **Die Theosophie F. Chr. Oetingers,** Tübingen 1847, p. 147ff.

163. Heinrich Knittermeyer, **Schelling und die romantische Schule,** München 1928, completely neglected to mention the mystical sources of German romantic philosophy; Eckhart, Boehme, Oetinger, Swedenborg and the cabala do not exist for him.

164. See Fritz Lieb, **Franz Baaders Jugendgeschichte. Die Frühentwicklung eines Romantikers,** München 1926, chapter 6; "Baader Und Saint-Martin. a) St. Martin und sein Lehrer Martinez de Pasqually," p. 143ff.

165. Papus (= Dr. G. Encausse), **M. de Pasqually, suivi des Catéchismes des Elus-Coëns,** Paris 1895, p. 120; see also Forgame, **De l'influence de l'esprit philosophique et de celle des sociétés secrètes sur le XVIIIe et le XIXe siècle.** Paris 1858; Auguste Viatte, **Les sources occultes du romantisme,** Paris 1928.

166. **Oeuvres posthumes,** I, p. 72, mr. 576.

167. Ibid., p. 23, nr. 165.

168. Ibid.

169. Ibid., p. 42, nr. 334.

170. Ibid., p. 102, c. 789: "In rereading some extracts of Swedenborg, I felt that he had more of what one calls the science of souls than the science of spirits; and in this respect, although he is not worthy to be compared to B(oehme) for real knowledge, it is possible that he is in accord with a great number of men: for B(oehme) suits only those who are entirely regenerated or, at least, those who would like to be so."

171. Saint-Martin was introduced to Swedenborg's doctrine in England (1782) by the members of the "New Jerusalem." In 1783, he met Silverhjelm, the nephew of Swedenborg; it was under his personal influence that he published **Nouvel Homme** and **Ecce Homo.**

172. On Strasbourg, see Saint-Martin, **Mon Portrait Historique et philoso-phique 1789-1803,** published by Robert Amadou, Paris 1961, p. 90 nr. 118.

> The city of Strasbourg is the second after Bordeaux to which I owe an inestimable debt, because it is there that I became acquainted with the precious truths, whose seeds Bordeaux had already provided for me. And it was through my dear friend, that they came to me, because there I met my dear B(oehme)."

Also see **Cinq textes inédits de Louis-Claude de Saint-Martin,** published by Robert Amadou, p. 1, with a preface of the **Mysterium Magnum,** translated from Boehme's German, and with some of Saint-Martin's remarks on students of Boehme such as Gichtel, Tscheer, etc.

173. **La correspondence inédite de St. Martin et Kirchberger, baron de Liebistorf,** published by L. Schauer and A. Chuquet, Paris 1862, especially, pp. 28, 29, 42. On Kirchberger, see Paul Wernle, **Der schweizerische Protestantismus im XVIII. Jahrhundert,** Bd. III: **Religiöse Gegenströmungen. Die Ausstrahlungen der französischen Revolution auf Schweizer Boden,** Tübingen 1925, p. 210; see also the recently published work of Antoine Faivre, "Kirchberger et l'illuminisme du dix-huitième siècle" in **Archives Internationales d'Histoire des Idées,** 16, The Hague 1966, pp. 101ff., 206ff.

174. See Corr. inéd., pp. 43, 50.

175. There are still no studies on the influence of Schwenkfeld and Valentin Weigel in France. On Schwenkfeld in Italy, see George Williams' excellent book, **The Radical Reformation,** London 1962, p. 541ff.

176. Paul Wernle, **Der schweizerische Protestantismus III,** p. 211.

177. On Pasqually, see note 165.

178. Marburg/Lahn, Hofstatt II.

179. Corr. inéd., p. 159ff.

180. On the beginnings of the Academy of Berlin, see Jean Henry

Samuel Formey, **Histoire de l'Académie Royale des Sciences et Belles Lettres depuis son origine jusqu'à présent, avec les pièces originales,** Berlin 1750, 2nd ed. augm., Berlin 1752; Carlo Denina, "De l'influence qu'a eue l'Académie de Berlin sur d'autres grands éstablissements de la même nature," **Mémoires. 1792–1793,** p. 562–73; Christian Bartholomèss, **Histoire philosophique de l'Académie de Prusse depuis Leibniz jusqu'à Schelling, particulièrement sous Frédéric le Grand,** tomes 1 and 2, Paris 1850–51; Emil Du Bois-Reymond, **Die Berliner Französische Kolonie in der Akademie der Wissenschaften, Festrede, Sitz,** Ber. 1886, I, pp. 317–30, also in Du Bois-Reymond, **Reden,** Folge 2, Leipzig 1887, p. 503–34; 2nd ed. t. 2, Leipzig 1912, p. 301–320.

181. There are no modern studies on the contribution of the Academy of Berlin, founded by Leibniz, to French literature and civilization; the official language of the Academy was French until the reform introduced by Wilhelm von Humboldt in 1806; and many first-rate French scholars were members of the Academy. Many independent French thinkers took part in the meetings of the Academy, as the case of Saint-Martin shows; cf. Saint-Martin, **Oeuvres posthumes,** t. II, p. 3.

182. Ibid., p. 3f.

183. Ibid., p. 4.

184. Ibid., p. 349.

185. Young's work was well-known, especially in the German and Russian freemasonry circles; see J. L. Kind, **Edward Young in Germany,** 1906.

186. On Edward Young's influence on Klopstock, see Gerhard Kaiser, **Klopstock, Religion und Dichtung,** Gütersloh 1963, pp. 42, 136, 185, 312; in the ode "An Young" Klopstock calls him "Widerleger der Freigeister."

187. Klopstock, **Oden,** hgg. von F. Muncher and J. Pawel, Stuttgart 1889, Bd. II, p. 63.

188. See Ernst Benz, "Russische Eschatologie (Jung-Stilling und Solowjew)" in **Kyrios, Vierteljahrsschrift für Kirchen und Geistesgeschichte Osteuropas,** 1936, pp. 102–29; also by the same author, **Jung-Stilling in Marburg,** Marburg/Lahn 1949, p. 20f.

189. Klopstock, **Oden,** Bd. 11, p. 72.

190. **Oeuvres posthumes,** I, p. 19, nr. 127.

191. P. Wernle, **Der schweizerische Protestantismus III,** p. 282; see Langmesser, **J. Sarasin,** 1899.

192. P. Wernle, **Der Schweizerische Protestantismus, III,** p. 283.

193. **Fr. A. Jacobis auserlesener Briefwechsel,** 2 Bde, ed. by Friedrich Roth, Leipzig 1827, Bd. II, p. 309.

194. Ibid., p. 310.

195. Schwenkfeld was the favorite mystic of a circle of Protestant gentlemen in Bohemia and Silesia; see Selina Gerhard Schultz, **Caspare Schwenkfeld von Ossig,** Norristown, Pa., 1947.

196. Ph. Schwartz, **Der erste Kulturkampf in Preussen um Kirche und Schule (1788-98),** 1925; F. Valjavec, "Das Wöllnersche Religionsedikt und seine geschichtliche Bedeutung," in **Historisches Jahrbuch der Görres-Gesellschaft** 72, 1953, pp. 386-400; on Wöllner, see **Allgemeine Deutsche Biographie,** Bd. 44, p. 148ff.

197. R. Le Forestier, **Les Illuminés de Bavière et la Franc-maçonnerie Allemande,** Paris 1915; Leopold Engel, **Geschichte des Illuminaten-Ordens,** 1906; G. Schuster, **Die geheimen Gesellschaften II,** 1906, p. 144ff.; A. Kluckhohn, **Die Illuminaten und die Aufklärung in Bayern, I,** 1869 in **Vorträge und Aufsätze,** 1894, p. 313ff.

198. Adam Weishaupt, **Vollständige Geschichte der Illuminaten in Bayern,** 1786; **Apologie der Illuminaten,** 1786; **System des Illuminatenordens,** 1787.

199. See Adolph Freiherr von Knigge, **Über den Umgang mit Menschen, Ausgewählt und eingeleitet von Iring Fetscher,** Fischer-Bücherei, Bücher des Wissens 1962; Karl Gödecke, **Adolph Freiherr Knigge,** Hannover 1844; Reinhold Th. Grabe, **Das Geheimnis des Adolph Freiherrn von Knigge, Die Wege eines Menschenkenners,** Hamburg-Leipzig 1936.

200. On Willermoz, see Papus, **Martinésisme, Willermozisme et Franc-maçonnerie,** Paris 1899; Louis de Combes, **Notes sur les illuminés,** p. 1 and q.

201. On Jakob Hermann Obereit (1725-98), see Th. Stettner, **Goethejahrbuch 17,** 1907, pp. 192-204; **Allgemeine Deutsche Biographie** and P. Wernle, **Schweizerischer Protestantismus III,** p. 215-221.

202. On the secret tradition of the idea of the "Unknown Philosopher," see Louis-Claude de Saint-Martin, **Pensées mythologiques. Cahier des langues, publié pour la première fois avec une étude sur le "Philosophe Inconnu" et les "philosophes inconnus"** by Robert Amadou, La Tour Saint-Jacques, cahier VII, Paris 1961.

203. Bode, **Examen impartial du livre intitulé Des Errerus et de la Vérité par un frère Laïque en fait des sciences,** o.O.

204. On Claudius, see Wolfgang Stammler, **Matthias Claudius, der Wandsbecker Bote, Beitrag zur deutschen Literatur- und Geistesgeschichte,** Halle/Saale 1915; Urban Roedl, **Matthias Claudius, Sein Weg und seine Welt,** Berlin 1934; C. Mönckeberg, **Matthias Claudius, Beitrag zur Kirchen- und Literaturgeschichte seiner Zeit,** 1869; F. Loofs, **Matthias Claudius in kirchengeschichtlicher Beleuchtung,** 1915; O. Dietz, **Matthias Claudius, der Mensch und seine Welt,** 1924.

205. See H. Düntzer, **Christoph Kaufmann,** Leipzig 1882, p. 278ff.; W. Stammler, **Matthias Claudius,** p. 151ff.

206. J. Pfeiffer, **Matthias Claudius, der Wandsbecker Bote, Eine Einführung in den Sinn seines Schaffens,** 1940, 6. Aufl. 1949 speaks of a "treuherzige Natürlichkeit."

207. As we found already in Joh. Albr. Bengel, see p. 40.

208. Matthias Claudius, **Vorrede** p. 111. Complete title: **Irrthümer und Wahrheit, oder Rückweis für die Menschen auf das allgemeine Principium aller Berkenntnis. Ein Werk, darin die Beobachter auf die Ungewissheit ihrer Untersuchungen und auf ihre beständige Fehltritte geführt werden, und ihnen solcher Weise der Weg angedeutet wird, den sie härten gehen müssen, um die physische Evidenz zu erhalten über den Ursprung des Guten und des Bösen, über den Menschen, über die materielle Natur, über die immaterielle Natur und die heilige Natur, über die Basis der politischen Regierungen, über die Autorität der Souverains, über die bürgerliche und peinliche Gerechtigkeit, über die Wissenschaften, die Sprachen und die Künste. Von einem unbek. Ph. Aus dem Französischen übersetzt, von Matthias Claudius. Mit Churfürstl. Sächsischem gnädigsten Privilegio.** Verlegt by Gottlieb Löwe in Breslau 1782.

209. Cf. note 178; the "signs of the times," see Matt. 16:3: "You are not able to discern the signs of the times."

210. The man of desire understood as the man tormented by nostalgia for the heavenly fatherland is already to be found in Joh. Gottlob Fichte's religious anthropology, **Die Anweisung zum seligen Leben, oder auch die Religionslehre, Sämmtl. Werke,** ed. by J. H. Fichte, Bd. 5, p. 409:

> Und so irret denn der arme Abkömmling der Ewigkeit, verstossen aus seiner väterlichen Wohnung, immer umgeben von seinem himmlischen Erbtheile, nach welchem seine schüchterne Hand zu greifen bloss sich fürchtet, unstät und flüchtig in der Wüste umher, allenthalben bemüht sich anzubauen; zum Glück durch den baldigen Einsturz jeder seiner Hütten erinnert, dass er nirgend Ruhe finden wird, als in seines Vaters Hause."

211. Lavater, see Fritz Lieb, **Franz Baaders Jugendgeschichte,** München 1926, p. 180f.

212. Herder, see Fritz Lieb, Ibid., p. 181; also see Herder, **Briefe an Hamann,** hgg. see Hoffmann, Berlin 1889, p. 168; Haym, **Herder,** Bd. II, p. 200.

213. Hamann, see Fritz Lieb, ibid., p. 182f.

214. Goethe, **Xenien,** 1798.

215. See **Goethe und Lavater,** hgg. v. F. B. Zürich 1918, p. 56.

216. See note 203.

217. Mit Churfürstl. Sächsischen allergnädigsten Privilegio, Hamburg

und Leipzig bey H. I. Matthiessen, 1790.

218. On St. Martin, vol. 53.

219. <u>Berliner Monatsschrift</u>, August 1795, p. 160.

220. Franz Xaver Bronner of Augsburg wrote to Sailer (Aug. 24, 1786):

Ich war noch nicht lange in Augsburg, als Herr von Lütgen-
dorf (am 24 Aug. 1786) mit einem grossen Aerostaten
die Luft beschiffen wollte und sich mit ausserordentlicher
Feierlichkeit dem Volke dieses Schauspiel zu geben an-
schickte. Die Begierde, den Luftballon steigen zu sehen,
hatte eine ausserordentliche Menge Fremder nach Augsburg
gelockt. Unter anderem waren auch die Professoren Sailer
und Weber dahin gekommen (aus Dillingen) und pflegten
bald mit Herrn Provikar (de Haiden), bald mit meinem
Hausherrn Critolaus (d.i., Konrad Schmid) und anderen
Herren in Augsburg vertraulichen Umgang. Critolaus machte,
seiner Geschäfte wegen als Rechtsfreund verschiedener
Parteien, mehrmals kleine und grössere Reisen, und ich
bemerkte, dass ihm Sailer bei solchen Anlässen mündlich
oder schriftlich öfters einige Aufträge oder Anweisungen
gab; was die Aufträge eigentlich betrafen, konnte ich
kaum ein paarmal erforschen; die Anweissungen waren
Empfehlungen an Freunde usw. Dass Critolaus noch immer
Freimaurer sei und zwar vom sogenannten alten System,
und dass er in Augsburg das Amt eines Meisters vom
Stuhl bekleide, verhehlte er mir gar nicht, sondern nahm
sich vielmehr bei jeder Gelegenheit die Mühe, mich für
den damals herausgekommenen 'Hirten-brief an die Freimaurer des alten Systems' eine Art Rosenkreuzer, für
das Buch 'des erreurs et de la vérité' (von Louis Claude
de Saint-Martin), sogar für ein Büchlein Jakob Böhmes,
dessen Titel ich vergessen habe, überhaupt aber für alles
Mystische einzunehmen . . . Es konnt ihm nicht entgehen,
dass ich eine unüberwindliche Abneigung gegen alle Mystik
und ein sichtbares Misstrauen gegen alle geheimen Wissenschaften im Herzen nährte; dennoch liess er mir solange
keine Ruhe, bis ich endlich aufgebracht und in derbem
Tone erklärte, ich wolle mich durchaus nicht mehr am
Gängelbande geheimer Obern, vielleicht gar versteckter
Jesuiten führen lassen.

221. Joh. Aug. Starck, **Über Krypto-Katholizismus, Proselytenmacherei,
Jesuitismus, geheime Gesellschaften**, I. Theil, Frankfurt-Leipzig 1787, Nachtrag über
den Kryptokatholizismus, Giessen 1788.

222. On Starck, see also G. Krüger in **Festgabe für Karl Müller**, Tübingen
1922; Jean Blum, **J. A. Starck et la querelle du cryptocatholicisme en Allemagne**,
Paris 1914.

223. **Krypto-Katholizismus**, I, p. 148.

224. Ibid., II, p. 139.

225. Ibid., p. 280. The same kind of hostile criticism is found in a letter of Baron George de Cuvier, the celebrated naturalist, to his friend, Joh. Friedr. Pfarr, the famous mathematician (1769-1832), from Caen, Oct. 14, 1788:

> "I wish to speak to you about a book which if it is not new (it was published in 1782), is nonetheless rare and strange. Perhaps you have heard of the Martinists? It is a sect of dreamers who, for several years, have been infiltrating everywhere and are especially capable of imposing upon grand lords in the most impertinent manner-- Cagliostro belongs to this sect--Cardinal de Rohan and the King of Prussia, Frederick William, are its most notable adherents. Their system is contained in this book, the title of which is **Des erreurs et de la vérité ou les hommes rappellés aux principes de la science par un Ph. inc. 1782.**
>
> Now listen to this string of absurdities. After a lot of philosophical nonsense about our evil state, about the principle of good and bad, he comes to the cause of this misfortune. Man's number, when God created him, was 4. Now he has fallen to 3; and in order for man to become happy again, he must get back up to the number 4. Here is the proof: the number of the circumference of a circle and each curved line is 3; the number of the radius and of each straight line is 4; but if there were no circumference, the radius could be stretched out to infinity, and similarly our minds would have no limits, if we were not at number 3. But even better is this proof by numbers: a circumference is, we may say, a zero (0), for both are round, in the middle is the center which is simple and everywhere equal to 1; now 1 and 0 make 10; consequently, each circle is equal to 10. To determine the value of the circumference, it is necessary to subtract the value of the center from that of the entire circle; and as 10 - 1 = 9, who can doubt that the value of the circumference is equal to 9? Q.E.D. You would not believe that anyone could write such nonsense; but that is nothing; let us continue. Here is why the number of the radius is equal to 42: The radius is the side of a triangle which can be inscribed in a circle. Now all triangles, as everyone knows, = 3; if to this number, we add the center, which is equal to 1, we obtain the following result: the radius = 3 + 1 = 4; a stronger demonstration is one which demonstrates proof that there are 360 degrees in a circle. We can inscribe in each circle 6 triangles of equal sides.

128

Each of these triangles = 3; so put down 3; and as there are 6 of these triangles, write 6, which makes 36. In third place, comes the circumference, which, as we have seen = 0, which makes 360. Q.E.D. Well, who would dare to contend that the number 360 was arbitrary? The same goes for the principles of physics; only 3 elements are recognized, because everything proceeds by 3, for otherwise everything would be eternal, because the number 4 is invariable because of its perfection. The 3 elements are fire, water, and earth, or what amounts to the same, sulphur, salt, and mercury. Sulphur and salt are enemies; but mercury unites and combines them by separating them one from the other, etc. It is this strange repertory of nonsense that the Martinists regard as their Bible. Each of them works to understand it and they treat as profane those who see it at its real value, that is to say, as the product of a disorganized brain. I would never have believed it if I had not seen it. An officer of the regiment in the town who studied it with care became mad. One day, when he was at church, he threw himself face down on the ground and stayed for a quarter hour in this position; on leaving he noticed the gargoyle; he took it for St. Peter and gave it three francs. He thought a beggar was the Holy Virgin and gave her 6 francs. Finally, he took a beggar for J. C. (Jesus Christ) and gave him his watch. The beggar saw what was happening and took the watch to the colonel, who had the officer taken to his quarters with orders to keep him out of sight. The officer remained unconscious for three hours; and upon his coming to, he wrote: 'I was at mass in Rouen.' A little later, he became enraged and cried: 'Here I am at 4.' Although at 4, he would have thrown himself out the window if four strong soldiers had not restrained him. Here are the effects of faulty instruction. If he had had in his head one single grain of logic of geometry, St. Martin would not have been able to have an effect on him. All that I have just told you is the bare truth. I have read this book, and the facts were related to me by the captain of Surville . . .

Caen, Sept. 22, 1789:

I would like you to acquaint me with the German studies, especially those of Berlin; detailed information of Martinism, crypto-Catholicism, etc., would be most welcome; you are on a great stage, and such doctrines often have the greatest effect on the course of politics.

(The extracts from these two letters were graciously shared with me by Mlle. Droz at the end of my lectures on Saint-Martin at the College of France, with the right of publication.)

226. On August Neander (1789-1850) see **Allgemeine Deutsche Biographie,** Bd. 32, p. 33; Adolf von Harnack, "Rede auf August Neander 1889," in **Reden und Aufsätze** I, 1904, pp. 193-218; K. H. Schneider, **August Neander,** 1894; H. Hüttmann, August Neander in seiner Jugendentwicklung, Diss., Heidelberg 1936.

227. This sentence by Saint-Martin is found again in Baader, **Sämmtl. Werke,** Bd. II, pp. 72, 233, 422; cf. Saint-Martin, **Des erreurs,** pp. 12, 88; **Tableau naturel,** pp. 12, 173.

228. The similarity between the styles of Saint-Martin and Hamann merits close examination.

229. See **Des französischen Philosophen L. Cl. de St. Martin nachge-lassenen Werke. Aus der Urschrift und mit Anmerkungen von D. W. A. Schickedanz, K. Militair-Ober-Prediger, Ritter, etc.** Erster Theil: Die theosophischen Gedanken. Münster 1833, p. 7.

230. Schickedanz, **Biographischer Abriss,** pp. 202-204.

231. Ibid., p. 214.

232. Ibid., p. 212.

233. Baader took the French text of the **XL Questions sur l'Ame de Boehme,** in Saint-Martin's translation (Paris 1807), as the basis of his commentary, **Sämmtl. Werke,** Bd. 12, p. 469ff.

234. **Portrait of M. de Saint-Martin par lui-même,** published in extracts in Médecine de France, nr. 34, p. 38; **Oeuvres posthumes,** I, p. 1-139.

235. On Bishop Sailer, see Hubert Schiel, **Johann Michael Sailer, Leben und Briefe,** Bd. I, Leben und Persönlichkeit in Selbstzeugnissen, Gesprächen und Erinnerungen der Zeitgenossen, Regensburg 1948; Bd. II, Briefe, mit Bibliographie und Register zu Bd. I und II, Regensburg 1952. In Germany, Saint-Martin himself was put among the "Catholic romantics"; Hoffmann writes in the introduction to Vol. III of Franz Baader's works, 1852, p. lxvii:

> So brachte ganz kürzlich noch die Augsburger Allgemeine Zeitung in der Beilage zu nr. 200 (1852) einen Artikel über Anton Günther, in welchem dieser geniale Denker zu der Gruppe der katholischen Romantiker gerechnet wird, an deren Spitze Franz von Baader stehe; ausser St. Martin, Friedr. Schlegel, Z. Werner, J. Görres und Windischmann zählt jener Artikel auch Staudenmaier und Sengler unter diese katholischen Romantiker.

Hoffmann himself severely criticized this term.

236. Fritz Blanke, "Bishof Sailer und Johann Caspar Lavater, Ein Aus-schnitt aus der Geschichte des okumenischen Gedankens" in Zwingliana, Bd. IX, Heft 7, 1952, nr. 1, p. 431ff.

237. Ernst Benz, "Die abendländische Sendung der östlich-orthodoxen Kirche," **Abhandlungen der Akademie der Wissenschaften u.d. Literatur Mainz, Geistes- und sozialwiss. Klasse,** Bd. 8, Jg. 1950; Hildegard Schaeder, "Die dritte Koalition und die Heilige Allianz" in **Osteuropäische Forschungen,** NF 19, 1934.

238. H. Dalton, **Johannes Gossner,** 1873; third ed. 1898; H. Lockies, **Johannes Gossner,** 1936; second ed. 1956; W. Holsten, **Johannes Evangeliste Gossner,** 1949.

239. Hubert Schiel, **J. M. Sailers Briefe,** Regensburg 1952, p. 356; Sailer to Friedrich Karl von Savigny, Landshut, Dec. 16, 1810. Sailer wrote on his "Brosamen":

> Nr. 3 soll auf Saint Martin aufmerksam machen, der die Ansicht hat . . . Die Werke von Saint-Martin kannst Du in München nicht mehr haben. Ein Freund in Mannheim lieferte sie mir alle durch Fontaine, Buchhändler.

See the sentence by Saint-Martin cited in "Brosamen" (nr. 27):

> Der Mensch der Erde, Die Erze, in der Erde begraben, empfangen kein Licht. Die Pflanzen auf der Oberfläche der Erde empfangen Licht, aber sehen es nicht, und können sich desselben nicht freuen. Die Tiere empfangen, sehen es und werden dessen froh. Der Mensch empfängt das Licht, sieht es, kann sich dessen freuen und noch darüber nachsinnen, wo es herkomme. Hier liegt die Wurzel des Adels, den die jetzige Menschheit vor den übrigen Geschöpfen der Erde noch hat.

240. Letter to Friedrich Karl von Savigny, Landshut, July 2, 1811 in Schiel, **Briefe,** p. 373 (Brief nr. 359):

> Was und wieviel die Bücher von Saint-Martin kosten, weiss ich nicht; in München sind sie nicht mehr zu haben. Buchhändler Lafontaine in Mannheim liefert sie Dir alle, aber sehr teuer. Ich habe das **Ecce Homo** um einen Gulden 12 Kreuzer gekauft; die übrigen wurden mir geschenkt. Ausser den **Ministère de l'Homme-Esprit,** I. Band "de l'Esprit des Choses" (2 Bände) habe ich jetzt alle ausgelehnt."

241. On Lutterbeck, see **Allgemeine Deutsche Biographie,** Bd. 19, p. 707-708.

242. On Georg Hermes (1775-1831), see K. Werner, **Geschichte der katholischen Theologie,** 1889; and K. Schweiler, **Die zwei Wege der neueren Theologie,** 1926; H. Schroers, **Die Kölner Wirren,** 1927, p. 336ff; S. Merkle, "Der hermesian- ische Streit im Lichte neuer Quellen," **Historisches Jahrbuch der Görres-Gesellschaft** 60, 1940, pp. 179-200.

243. There is still no study of Chateaubriand in Germany. Several literary indications are found in the articles by F. Baldensperger on "Les deux

rencontres manquées entre Goethe et Chateaubriand," by Ch. Dédéyan, "Goethe et Chateaubriand," and by J. M. Carré, "L'Allemagne, la France et l'Angleterre en face de Goethe" in the Revue de Littérature Comparée dédiée à Goethe et Chateaubriand, Année 23, 1949, nr. 2-3; cf. also, Pierre Moreau, "Horizons internationaux de Chateaubriand," Revue de Littérature Comparée, t. 23, 1949, p. 257-286.

German translations of the **Génie du Christianisme** are as follows:

> 1) **Genius des Christentums oder Schönheit der christlichen Religion mit Anm. von** K(arl Heinrich Georg) Venturini, t. 1-4, Münster, Theyssing 1803-04, 4°; 2) **Die Schönheiten des Christentums oder Religion und Gottesdienst der Katholiken,** Solothurn-München, Weber, 1280; 3) **Die Schönheiten des Christentums, oder: Religions-und Gottesdienst der Katholiken,** Mainz, Müller, 1828; 4) **Geist des Christentums,** übers v. Hermann Kurtz, Abt. 1-3. Ulm, Heerbrandt u. Thämel, 1844; 5) **Der Geist des Christentums,** übers v. J. F. Schneller, 2. nach der neuesten Orig.-Ausgabe rev. Aufl. besorgt durch J. König Bd. 1-2, Freiburg i. Br., Wagner, 1856; 1875.

244. Lutterbeck, **Einleitung,** p. VIII-IX Lutterbeck was the author of **Sach-und Namen-Register mit Einleitung über Entwicklungsgang und System der Baaderschen Philosophie,** = Sämmtl. Werke, Bd. XVI, 1860.

245. **Ministère de l'homme-esprit,** p. 368ff.; the sentences cited were omitted in the German translation!

246. Lutterbeck, **Einleitung,** p. X.

247. On Friedrich von Schlegel, see F. Imle, **Friedrich von Schlegels Entwicklung von Kant zum Katholizismus,** 1927; Benno von Wiese, **Friedrich Schlegel,** 1927; K. A. Horst, **Ich und Gnade, Eine Studie über Friedrich Schlegels Bekehrung,** 1951; E. Bohle, **Friedrich von Schlegel,** 1956.

247a. A typical judgment on Schlegel's conversion is found in P. G. van Ghert's letter to Hegel, a postscript to his Amsterdam letter, Feb. 25, 1811 (**Briefe,** Bd. I):

> PS: Ist es wirklich wahr, wie man hier erzählt, dass Fr. Schlegel in Wien so bigottkatholisch geworden ist, dass er nichts tut als beten?--non credidero.

248. See W. Schütz, **Joh. Friedr. Kleuker, seine Stellung in der Religionsgeschichte des ausgehenden 18 Jahrh.,** 1927.

249. Franz von Baader, **Sämmtl. Werke,** Bd. 12, p. 241.

250. Ibid., Bd. 15, p. 188ff.

251. Franz von Baader's **Bemühungen um den Nachlass von St. Martin.**

252. Franz von Baader, Bd. XV, **Brief** nr. 66, p. 307.

253. On Johann Konrad Pfenniger, see P. Wernle, **Der schweizerische Protestantismus** III, p. 285ff.; and G. R. Zimmermann, **Joh. Konr. Pfenniger, ein christlicher Apologete**, Züricher Taschenbuch 1881. Pf. publia Das Christliche Magazin 1779-1780; Sammlungen zu einem christlichen Magazin 1781-1783; das Repertorium für denkende Bibelverehrer aller Konfessionen, 1784; his collaborators were Lavater, Häfeli, Stolz, Kleuker, Wizenmann (Oetinger's student) and Phil. Matth. Hahn, also a pupil of Oetinger. Lavater dedicated his book to his departed friend, **Etwas über Pfenniger.**

254. Sammlungen zu einem christlichen Magazin, Bd. II, Heft 2, 1782, p. 193ff., and Bd. IV, Heft 2, 1784, pp. 187-223.

255. Franz von Baader, **Tagebuch**, Weiern, Jan. 31, 1787; **Sämmtl. Werke**, Bd. II, p. 126f.

256. Franz von Baader, **Tagebuch**, München, May 7, 1787; **Sämmtl. Werke**, Bd. II, p. 147f.

257. In Vol. XII of **Sämmtl. Werke**, München, p. 141ff.

258. Ibid., Bd. II, pp. 125-136.

259. Ibid., Bd. 15, p. 240ff.

260. Ibid., p. 241.

261. **Oeuvres posthumes**, I, p. 122, nr. 1031.

262. Ibid., p. 64, nr. 458.

263. Ibid., p. 128, nr. 1090.

264. Ibid., p. 109, nr. 906.

265. Schickedanz, p. 209.

266. **Oeuvres posthumes**, I, p. 137, nr. 1135.

267. Ibid., p. 96, nr. 743.

268. Ibid., p. 40, nr. 319.

269. Ibid., p. 48, nr. 362.